MID-MICHIGAN HISTORY

THE MT. PLEASANT AREA'S PAST

AS SEEN IN THE MORNING SUN

& MT. PLEASANT MONTHLY
MAGAZINE FEATURES
WITH BONUS PAGES!

By Jack R. Westbrook

Copyright 2013 by Jack R. Westbrook
ISBN: 10- 09484036148
ISBN 13/EAN 13 9780984036141

Published by ORSB Publishing
POB 16 Mount Pleasant, Michigan, 48804-0016
989-773-5741

Dedicated to the loyal fans of the Michigan Monthly Magazine "The Way We Were" feature and the Morning Sun Mid-Michigan History series that began in 2010 and to my wife, Mary Lou, who suggested this book.

THE COVER: A 1937 view of downtown Mt. Pleasant from the air, believed to be the first taken from an airplane and further believed to be taken from the airplane of Mt. Pleasant Walter J. McClanahan, an early advocate of private aircraft.

INTRODUCTION

In case we haven't met in person or in print.

My people came to Mt. Pleasant in the early 1930s from Logan, Ohio, as part of the rush of humanity who came to mid-Michigan because the 1928-discovered Mt. Pleasant oil field had triggered a rush to jobs here during the Great Depression.

I was almost literally born in the oil fields of Michigan. My Dad and Granddad were drilling a hole in the Columbia Field just outside Bloomingdale, Michigan (about 20 miles northwest of Kalmazoo),when my Dad met my Mother, a rural Bloomingdale girl. They married in 1938 and I arrived the first of February,1940, in South Haven, Michigan, when both had just come from another well they were drilling. In those days you often were your own drilling crew and Mom worked alongside Dad the day of the night I was born.

I was pretty much raised in Mt. Pleasant.

A horrendous automobile accident nearly cost me my father, who was in a coma for more than a month when I was less than three years old. When he came out of the coma, his nerves were shot, so he became a short order cook while my grandfather became a machinist and mechanic first for Simrall Pipeline Company and then for Union Rotary drilling contractors,

My love of putting ink on paper began when my sixth grade student teacher, Jack Anson (later Assistant Superintendent of Mt. Pleasant Schools) inspired us kids to start a student newspaper. Later, at Mt. Pleasant High School, English and Journalism teacher Tom Northway encouraged me to write for *The Stude*, a by-monthly student newspaper. I wrote, sold ads in and edited across four years of high school.

I joined the Navy to be a Journalist, so of course they put me in an electronics rate.

Most of my post-Navy work career has involved publishing, first as a newspaper advertising salesman, then ad manager, then as a copywriter for Ray Cline Marketing, a Mt. Pleasant advertising agency.

In 2003, I went to work for *the Michigan Oil & Gas News* magazine, first as General Manager, then as Managing Editor. That career lasted nearly 28 years, until an accident on an outside staircase sent me foot-first to a paved parking lot, shattering my right ankle joint and breaking both big and little bones in my leg. I wrote from home for awhile, then was a part-timer and finally semi-retired in 2001, fully retiring at the end of 2007.

I do not retire well.

Along the way I had accumulated almost 20,000 images of the historic Michigan oil and gas industry and the Mt. Pleasant area.

I put my first book on the streets in 2006 and, with this, will have written ten (nine photo histories and a historical novel) books of my own, plus one commissioned autobiography, one oil & gas exhibit catalogue for the 2005 exhibit at the Clrake Historical Library on the Mt. Pleasant campus of Central Michigan University, and edited formatting of another personal memoir for a friend.

I did a monthly "The Way We Were" local historical feature for the now defunct Mt. Pleasant Monthly Magazine (December, 2007 to December 2012) and since June of 2010 have written "Mid-Michigan History", a regular feature in Mt. Pleasant's Morning Sun daily newspaper.

Recently at book signings, we've hear a number of people say "I wish I'd saved some of your articles". In late November, my wife said "You should think about doing a book of all of your columns." I didn't just think about it, I did it in a week.

So here it is, all of my historical columns plus a few bonus pages, some never before published, some from my other books. Enjoy!

Jack R. Westbrook
December 3, 2013

Middle Michigan …. A place for New Beginnings

The story of Isabella County in the center of the Michigan Lower Peninsula "mitten" is a story of new beginnings.

The area now known as Isabella County was home to abundant majestic pine and hardwood trees, one of the best such forests in the Great Lakes region. Known among the Indians as "Ojibiway Besse" (the place of the Chippewa), part of the area of present day Isabella County was their winter hunting grounds and may have been used by American Indians for more than 10,000 years. Europeans are comparatively recent arrivals. Father Marquette's successor Father Henry Nouvel spent a winter here in 1675 with the Beaver Clan of the Chippewa Indians. Nearly two centuries later, Europeans returned to the middle of Michigan and the area we know as Isabella County to harvest the verdant forests to supply the growing appetite for building materials as the nation flourished.

The contrast between the nomadic life of the Indians and the agricultural and commerce nature of the European settlers brought about new beginnings for both. In 1885 a treaty was signed between the U.S, government and seven Michigan Indian tribes, including the Chippewa, setting aside in trust the land encompassed by the present Chippewa Indian Reservation. The treaty also removed from general sale lands in parts of six present-day Isabella County townships for a period of time, those lands available for purchase only by Indians. Those lands unpurchased by Indians went back on the general market a few years later. With nothing here to sustain them, "indian mills" were built to enable them to grind corn and Indians began gathering there, as did merchants. Indian Mills became Isabella City, then Isabella Center. Also in 1855 Isabella County's first township, Coe, was established and John Hursh settled in the area near what would be the present day Mount Pleasant.

Carved from contiguous named lands in 1831 legislative act, Isabella County was formally organized in 1859 by Act No. 118 of the Michigan Legislature officially established and organized Isabella County, with the county seat located Indian Mills, by then called Isabella City. Typical of European settlers who came here to farm in the aftermath of the lumber era was the John and Gertrude Gross family who settled on Weidman Road near today's Beal City. John Gross was born in the Eifel region of Germany in 1847, sailed to America and arrived in New York in 1868. He and his family lived in Westphalia, Michigan, before settling in the Michigan Upper Peninsula's Keewenaw Peninsula, where he worked with his father and brothers in copper mines. He and his brother settled, with their families, in Nottawa Township during the late 1880s. In the early 20th Century, the John and Gertrude

Gross family consisted of, *left to right; front center* – Minnie Gross; second row – Gertrude, Eva, John; and back row – Charlie, Michael, Joseph, Rosina, William, Leo and Ernie.

Another Isabella County new beginning commenced, "city life" as the village thrived with saw and grist mills and county government became an integral part of Mt. Pleasant life. A wooden courthouse was built in 1860 and in 1876 a grand Victorian-era styled courthouse was built, followed by a same-styled jail in 1880.

Passage of the Homestead Act of 1862 made new middle Michigan beginnings possible for many black settlers, now known as the "Old Settlers of Michigan", to begin a new life on homesteads in Isabella, Mecosta and Montcalm counties from Ontario, Canada and Ohio after successfully escaping slavery via the Underground Railway. The first African American settlers went into Rolland Township that year in 1862. In 1904, 60 Isabella County farms were African American owned.

Besides clearing land, homesteading and farming, many of the Old Settler's of Michigan African American men found work in the burgeoning lumber camps of Isabella County in the latter half of the 19th Century. At the Jolett Lumber Camp, in Rolland Township, In

Broomfield Township, the Bundy Lumber Company Camp # 4 crew, with William Dow as foreman, posed with a sled load of logs totaling an estimated astounding 7,672 board feet. As was often the case with such photographs, the estimated board feet of a log was hand lettered on the end of that pictured log.

While commerce and settlement flourished in the area another new beginning was born of educational necessity. Each year in August, the teachers of Isabella County would conduct their annual "institute". During that time a test was given to high school graduates applying for teachers credentials and, if passed, teaching certificates were issued. During the teacher's institute of 1892, the failure rate among those taking the teachers test was so high that it was determined that a "normal" (school devoted to training teachers) was needed. The Central Michigan Normal and Business Institute opened on the second floor of the Carpenter Building in downtown Mt. Pleasant in the autumn. Meantime, the Mount Pleasant Development Company was established by local businessmen sold 224 lots for $10 each, leaving a ten acre plot in the southern part of town for the Central Michigan Normal and Business Institute, which became a state teacher's training school in 1895. The Central Normal School campus, shown in this 1910 postcard view, remains the nucleus of what is now Central Michigan University, fourth largest university in the state with 27,000 student enrollment, 19,000 at the home 258 acre home campus.

The third oil field discovered after Michigan became a commercially producing oil state at Saginaw in 1925 was the 1927 Mount Pleasant Field at Chippewa Township of Isabella County. Pure Oil Company built a "village" for its workers and the Mt. Pleasant Field was born. This new beginning brought people throughout the nation to central Michigan, bringing prosperity to the area with petroleum royalty revenue to landowners, worker payroll to merchants and a housing shortage, all of which would serve the area in good stead when the devastation of the Great Depression of 1929 plunged the nation into financial turmoil for a decade. In 1935 the Michigan Oil and Gas Exposition drew more than 25,000 people to Mt. Pleas ant's Island Park. A parade initializing the Exposition was led by a mock hearse containing an effigy of "Ole Man Depression" symbolizing industry activity having shielded the area from the financial devastation of the Great Depression.

To date 1,647 wells have been drilled in Isabella County in the search for oil and gas, resulting in 563 dry holes, 839 oil wells and 176 natural gas wells in 42 fields that have produced more than 46 million barrels of oil and 38 billion cubic feet of natural gas all time through 2006. The Michigan Oil and Gas Association was formed in Mount Pleasant in 1934, another new beginning, and the city is the "Oil Capital" of Michigan, named for being hub of oilfield action and commerce for eight decades. Presently, Michigan is 12th largest producer of natural gas and 17th largest producer of crude oil of the 34 United States producing oil and gas.

In 1957, Winn resident the late Norval Morey perfected and patented a tree debarking machine and Morbark industries was born, with the early prototypes fabricated in this blacksmith shop at Winn. The Morbark name has gained international fame and the expanding line of forest harvesting products combined with a corresponding growth of the headquarters factory and offices, just outside Winn in Section 15, Fremont Township.

So while the new beginning that was Isabella County started as a timber center a century and a half ago, the area is still known worldwide as a center for forest harvesting equipment through the local family of forestry machinery manufacturers comprised of Morbark industries and Bandit Industries.

The Chippewa Indian Tribe, whose nomadic lifestyle faced new beginnings as "citified" residents, acclimated to the white man's ways through training at the Indian Industrial School from 1893-1933, began anew as a major financial citizen of the community in the 1980s. The Soaring Eagle Resort and Casino is now the largest employer in Isabella County and many a public good project has had a new beginning thanks to the Chippewa Tribes grant distributions to local entities.

Treaty of 1855 establishes Indian Mills village and reservation.

In 1855 Isabella County's first township, Coe, was established and John Hursh settled in the area near what would be the present day Mount Pleasant. In 1859, Act No. 118 of the Michigan Legislature officially established and organized Isabella County.

Also in 1855, a group of Methodist religious leaders from Lapeer County began pressuring the federal government to establish a permanent place for native Americans, mainly members of the Chippewa tribe, to live since settlement in Southern Michigan was intense and the tribe's nomadic, with no sense of personal land ownership, were beginning to be problematic

The Federal Treaty of 1855 set aside in trust the land where the current Saginaw Chippewa Indian Reservation is headquartered. The treaty also set aside parts of six Isabella townships to be removed from availability for sale to anyone but the Indians for a period of time, after which the lands were made available to the general public for sale. Reverend George Bradley founded a Methodist Mission about three miles northeast of the present downtown Mt. Pleasant, and here a grist mill was built in 1857 to allow the resident Indians to make a living. The settlement was first known as Indian Mills, then later was named Isabella City.

The north-south road passing through the only organized population center in the county, was literally "the road to the mission or, easier on the tongue, Mission Road.

A historical marker near the corner of Bamber and River Roads, reads, *"MICHIGAN REGISTERED HISTORICAL SITE: INDIAN CEMETERY. In the 1850s, the Methodist Episcopal (Indian) Church established the Bradley Mission School and Cemetery in this area. Only a few grave markers are visible, and it is not known how many Indians are buried here. The best-known Indian buried here was Chief Saw-Shaw-Wa-Na-Beece (1817-1868). As a leader of the Saginaw Swan Creek and Black River Band of Chippewa, he signed the Treaty of 1855, which set aside six adjoining townships of land in Isabella County for his tribe."*

In 1931, the Isabella County Daughters of the American Revolution dedicated a monument at the Chippewa River north of Mount Pleasant reading "Indian Mills 1857-1870. Near this spot stood the Council House where government agents met the Chippewa Indians" Second from the left is Chapter regent, Jessie Grambau, whose son Raymond and Indian School student David Green flanked the monument. Longwood was south side of the Chippewa River.

Why Do They Call It: SHEPHERD?

First settlement at the present site of Shepherd in Coe Township occurred in 1857, known as Salt River. A sawmill and flour mill were built by harnessing the waters of the Salt River at "the Corners". The first United States Post Office in Isabella County was established in the William Robbins home in 1857. The village was platted in 1866. The Ann Arbor Railroad depot, above with the Estee Grain Elevator, came through west of the original settlement in 1885 and Isaac N. Shepherd built an entire block of stone near the railroad and the village of Shepherd, which encompassed Salt River, was incorporated in 1887.

Fire destroyed a great deal of Salt River that year and Salt River was included in Shepherd. *Below*, Shepherd's main thoroughfare looking west along Wright Avenue from Second Avenue pre-1927, with the presence of electricity apparent by elaborate power lines.

Besides the aforementioned 1877 fire, downtown Shepherd suffered three more conflagrations, along the north side of Wright Avenue in 1888 and along the south side of the same avenue in 1927 and Jack Arndt's Garage on the northwest corner of Wright and Third in 1947. *Left*, note the famous Taylor Hotel, later called the Calkins House, a block from the train station at the northeast corner of Wright and Second streets.

So why do they call it … MOUNT PLEASANT?

One of the great mysteries to Mt. Pleasant newcomers and longtimers alike is "Why do they call it Mt. Pleasant?" A number of exotic theories exist but the truth is a pretty mundane tale. In order to know how the name Mt. Pleasant came to be, you first have to know a little about Isabella County.

John Hurst, right, his wife Elizabeth and their six children were the Mt. Pleasant area's first white residents in February, 1855, settling on a farm in the area that 37 years later would be subdivided and become the site of Central Normal School (now Central Michigan University).

One of Hurst's first overnight guests in the spring of 1855 was 33 year-old New York land and lumber speculator David Ward, left, who had recently purchased 200 acres of land along the Chippewa River. Also in 1855, the U.S. government, following the treaty of 1855, established Isabella County land in trust for seven Native American tribes, including the Saginaw Chippewa Indians. Indians began to gather at a settlement around a mission along the Chippewa River just north of present-day Mt. Pleasant where a grist mill was established to provide them a way to earn a living. The settlement became known as Indian Mills. In 1859, Isabella County was officially organized (after having been an uninhabited designated county territory since 1831) and Indian Mills became Isabella City, then Isabella Center, where the first county building was a log cabin..

Meantime, David Ward, destined to become Michigan's first lumber millionaire, had timbered off his property along the Chippewa River, and established an unplatted village with the name Mt. Pleasant because the topography of the area reminded him of his boyhood home of Mt. Pleasant, New York, this according to Isaac A, Fancher's 1911 opus "*Isabella County Past and Present*". Ward also donated a five acre lot for a courthouse in 1860, on the condition that the Isabella County seat move to Mount Pleasant from Isabella Center. Mt. Pleasant was made Isabella county seat in 1860 and a small wooden county building and courthouse was built on the north side of the present Isabella County building complex on North Main Street.

Ward sold the village to Harvey and George Morton, of New York, who platted and recorded it in February. 1864. Mt. Pleasant was incorporated as a village in 1875 and as a city in 1889. The downtown has thrived ever since, as witnessed by the 1890s photo looking east and south from Main and Broadway, above, and the early 1920's scene below, looking west from Broadway and University (then College) where horse and horseless carriages shared the downtown street.

THE MORNING SUN – February 25, 2013

Mt. Pleasant Village Presidents 1875-1889.

Mt. Pleasant was incorporated as a village in 1875 and became the City of Mt. Pleasant in 1889. Serving as President of the community during those interim years were: John Marshall 1875-76; Daniel H. Gilman 1877-79; John T. Leaton 1879-80; Irving F. Arnold 1880-81; Charles T. Russell 1881-82; John H. Harris 1882-83; George T. Granger 1883-84; Robert Coughlin 1884-85; Thomas Fordyce 1885-86; Douglas Halson 1886-87; John Kane 1887-88; John Kinney 1888-89; and Warner Churchill 1889.

FROM THE BIGPICTURE BOOK OF MT. PLEASANT MICHIGAN, 2010

Isaac Fancher Pionereering leader of Mt. Pleasant for 70 years

233 North Main is the site of the first Mt. Pleasant home Isaac A. Fancher built in 1863. Isaac Fancher was born September 30, 1833, in Montgomery, New York. He was married June 6, 1860, to Althea Preston at Java, New York, shortly after he left law school. After a stint of prospecting for silver in Nevada, the Fanchers returned from the west to Kilbourn City, Wisconsin, where his parents had moved from New York state. Shortly thereafter, his wife received word that her father, Albert Preston, brother Wallace, sister Ellen and her husband Samuel Woodworth, had moved to a tiny settlement in central Michigan named Mt. Pleasant, where Ellen was the first schoolteacher in the newly named Isabella County seat. Probably at the behest of Althea, the young Fancher family moved to Mt. Pleasant.

Isaac A. Fancher about 1900.

Lumberman David Ward had timbered off his 200 acre holdings on the high ground beside the Chippewa River beginning in 1856. In 1860, he platted a village and named it Mt. Pleasant because the area reminded him of his boyhood home in Pleasant Valley, and the high banks of the Chippewa River where his land was located was reminiscent of a small mountain. In 1860, Ward gave the new Isabella County government five acres if they would move the county seat to his village, which he then sold to George Morton, a New York investor, George's nephew Harvey Morton and wife Cordelia were sent to promote the new village.

When 30 year-old Isaac Fancher arrived in Mt. Pleasant on July 4, 1862, there were two houses.

A crude cabin served as the first County Building just south of Mr. Preston's home at the corner of Main and Chippewa streets. Harvey Morton, who was building a hotel at the corner of what is now Main and Broadway to house potential prospective buyers of lots in the new village, sold Isaac Fancher three lots along Main Street. Fancher suggested that a new survey be done since the original plat had not been registered. One of Fancher's first Mt. Pleasant jobs was conducting the first registered plat of the village.

The need for better roads, railroads, schools and businesses was apparent to him and he set about on what would be a 71 year upbuilding of Mt. Pleasant from a backwoods frontier people cluster to a city. He built a home catty-cornered from his father-in-law's house.

He played a key role in bringing a number of entities to town to enhance community growth, including: the railroads; Central Michigan Normal School (now Central Michigan University); and the United States Indian Schools to the city. He was interested in lumber mills and built the Fancher block, one of the town's first commercial buildings, at the southeast corner of Main and Broadway.

Fancher served terms in both the Michigan Senate and Michigan House of Representatives, as well as being Mayor of Mt. Pleasant, City Attorney, County Surveyor, and Michigan Road Commissioner.

Around 1900, he sold most of his business interests to focus on his legal career, distin- guishing himself as one of Middle Michigan's leading attorneys. Fancher Avenue in Mt. Pleasant, one of the city's principal north-south thoroughfares, is named for Isaac A. Fancher, as is Fancher Elementary School at 801 South Kinney Street.

When Fancher died at 101 years old on March 19, 1934, the *Isabella County Times* said "Mr. Fancher continued to manifest a keen interest in this community and its welfare to the time of his death."

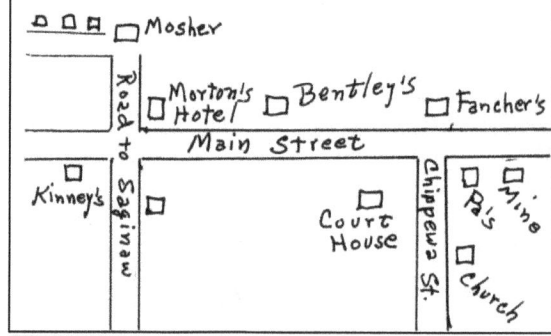

Ellen Woodworth's sketch of 1864 Mt. Pleasant, included in her letter to her husband Samuel when he was away in the Civil War.

Fancher's greatest legacy to the area, however, is his massive exhaustively detailed history book PAST AND PRESENT OF ISABELLA COUNTY MICHIGAN, published in 1911 by B. F. Bowen & Company of Indianapolis, Indiana. The best history of the county ever published and a seminal work for local historians, this rare 737 page illustrated volume details the history of the county and it's people in mind-boggling detail … a valued resource for this and other local history authors.

Fifty properties in and around Mt. Pleasant had deeds registered in Isaac Fancher's name over the years and records are obscure as to how long he occupied the 233 North Main address or the succession of home residents there until relatively recent times.

Following Fancher's death in 1934, the property was purchased by osteopathic Dr. R. A. Northway, who had come to Mt. Pleasant in 1910 and established offices first in the Dusenbury Building, then in the Exchange Bank Building, both downtown, before moving his practice to 233 North Main. He suspended operations of his clinic there about 1954, when failing health sent him to a convalescent home in Gladwin.

The property was vacant until May of 1958, when it was purchased by Peter and Anne Reale, ironically also from New York state, who rehabilitated the aging structure, adding on and operating a beauty salon at that location for many years before retiring there.

Two early views of Mt. Pleasant from the courthouse roof.

Two pictures of early Mt. Pleasant taken from the Isabella County Courthouse roof, looking south, three decades apart. Both photos capture the south side of Broadway Street looking toward High Street.

Above in early 1875, before fire wiped out most of the wooden buildings in the foreground, the St. James Hotel at the southwest corner of Broadway and Church *(now University)* Street dominates the scene. The huge white structure was created by Major Long when he moved two buildings from Isabella City (formerly Indian Mills) to this corner and covered them with a single roof. Just behind the St. James, the flat white building at the northwest corner of Church Street and Illinois Street is Mt. Pleasant's first schoolhouse. The row of buildings, center picture, on the south side of Broadway burned in 1882.

Below, in 1906 in the same scene looking down what was then Normal Street: the steeple of Sacred Heart Catholic Church can be seen upper left; the St. James Hotel has been replaced by the Commercial Building *(where Ace of Diamonds Jewelry is in modern times)*; and downtown buildings on both sides of Broadway are, for the most part, of brick construction.

Why Do They Call It: Blanchard?

In Section 16 of Rolland Township Phillip Blanchard bought an existing sawmill in 1876 and his P. G. Blanchard brought many to the area, prompting him to plat the village of Blanchard in 1879. In 1880, Phillip Blanchard sold more than 1,800 acres of timberland and his business to his sons and left the community. The community grew and was rebuilt after an 1884 fire. By 1891 there was no trace of the Blanchard family or their business in the area. For many years, the Dewitt Lumber Company on the millpond was the primary Blanchard business. In modern times, Blanchard was a shopping attraction, pioneered in the 1970s by Loafer's Glory, with several old buildings converted to vintage housewares, sundries, antiques and dining establishments.

Loafer's Glory closed in the final days of 2013.

Why Do They Call It: Winn?

Main Street Winn in Fremont Township is shown above in the early 1900s. The saga of the community's identity switch from Winn to Dushville and back to Winn is an odd tale. Originally an 1867 post office at the corner of Blanchard and Vandecar Roads was named Winn in honor of a pioneer's childhood home, Wynn, England. In 1878, the post office was moved a mile to the west to the village platted by William Dush, and renamed Dushville. When Dushville was originally platted, only south of Blanchard Road *(right in the top photo)*, carried that name while the area of the plat north of Blanchard Road *(left above)* was known as Hardscabble. Following William Dush's death, the name was changed back to Winn in 1898.

The Winn 50th Anniversary Celebration in 1917 featured a re-creation, *left*, in front of Starkweather's store on Main Street, of the weekly arrival of the mail courier. The mail carrier rode from Stanton in Montcalm County northeast to Mount Pleasant in Union Township, Isabella County, leaving Winn area mail in a wood box nailed to a tree a mile west of Winn.

NOTE: Winn photos' are courtesy Wayne Barrett, whose antique shop in Winn is located in the old Winn Masonic Temple.

Civil War Veterans "occupy" Dushville (Winn) in 1895.

On May 30, 1895, members of Herald Post Number 253, Department of Michigan Grand Army of the Republic (GAR), posed on Main Street in Dushville (Winn), Fremont Township. Left to right are: Berdett Caldwell, an unidentified drummer boy, Theodore Victory, Reverend Edwin R. Coburn, Lewis Priest, Warren Wind, Louis Schroder, George Osborn, Chris Reen, Doctor Mark H. Hillyard, Charlie Delo, Vet Johnson, Harry Brayton, Steve Smith, George Layman, Levi Little, George Doughty. Marshall Batchelder, Theodore Beuch, Elzy E. Dush, Jobe Priest, Thomas Williamson, George W. Foglesong and George Cullimore. (Photo courtesy of Wayne Barrett of Winn)

Why Do They Call It: Weidman?

In 1894, John S. Weidman came from his boyhood family farm in Mecosta County and bought timber lands in the Nottawa/Sherman county area to follow his father into the lumber business. He dammed the Coldwater River to float logs to his planing, saw and shingle mills and on July 4,. 1894 signed the plat establishing the village of Weidman's perimeters and streets. At the sawmill, John Weidman built a men's shanty and cookhouse for his mostly local workers. For the first year, Mrs. Weidman cooked for the workers, but as the operation grew, a men's cookhouse was constructed. John Weidman erected several businesses and donated lumber for a school to be built. He operated his mills for 16 years before selling out his interests in 1911.

The village of Weidman grew and prospered at the turn of the 20th Century. For several years after 1894, John Weidman's mills, produced about ten million board feet of lumber annually, prompting Mr. Weidman to persuade the Pere Marquette Railroad to the village to ship lumber, is shown below in 1908. Expanding his interests, John S. Weidman started the Weidman Banking Company around 1900 at Weidman and was also founder of the Isabella County State Bank at Mount Pleasant in 1902.

In 1905, Holmes Milling Company, was established in Weidman, building an elevator and mill powered by water shared from the mill pond built by John S. Weidman.

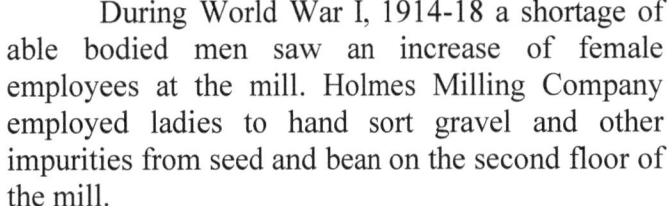

During World War I, 1914-18 a shortage of able bodied men saw an increase of female employees at the mill. Holmes Milling Company employed ladies to hand sort gravel and other impurities from seed and bean on the second floor of the mill.

The "beanpickers" Bloomer Girls basketball team, left, in the 1915-16 season included, *all left to right: back row* – Izora Wright, Hattie Dutcher and Theresa Kavanaugh; *middle row* - Ruth Taylor, Evalena Taylor and Hazel Parks; and *front* - Harriet McArthur.

The August 28, 1909 11th Annual Weidman "Fields Days", sponsored by Klondike brand Flour from local Holmes Milling Company feted townsfolk to a day of entertainment, festivities and "scoping out" the wares of vendors in street booths. Three years later, the event morphed into Weidman Days as the August 24, 1912 opening parade of now common automobiles wended its way down Main Street in front of Drallette's store. For several years, a highlight of Weidman life was the annual John Deere Days, sponsored by Charles Woolworth.

Why Do They Call It: Beal City?

A nameless settlement around a lumber camp starting in 1875, Beal City was unnamed for many years. In 1881 Nicholas Beal built the first general store and the first Beal City post office in the southeast corner of section 21, Nottawa Township, second building from the left above. Frank Vogel built the second store in Beal City in 1882, which would evolve into the Tilmann Hardware. The original Beal store was purchased in 1905 by Edward N. Smith, who added an annex for a meat market and built a tavern alongside the store in 1934. Smith sold to Walter Rau in 1945. In 1961, Rau moved the business to a more modern building across the street to and renamed the business Rau's Foodland.

Beal City is no stranger to Michigan governors. In July, 1908, Michigan Governor Fred M. Warner, driver's fender of the car, below, paused in front of Ed Smith's store campaigning in Beal City for re-election

Beal City High School graduate John Engler was elected a Michigan State Representative in 1971 and served 20 years in the Michigan legislature before 1991 election to the first of three terms as Michigan governor.

Why Do They Call It: Loomis?

The village of Loomis straddles the line between Sections 9 and 10 of Wise Township. The area began developing when Erastus Loomis, George Wise and E. F. Gould built a sawmill and general store there in 1871, clearing land, above, and platting a village then called Buchtel to greet the arrival of the Pere Marquette railroad line installed that same year. The post office opened as Buchtel in May of 1871 but the name was changed to Wise in December of that year and remained so named until closing in 1915. In 1872, Wise Township was named after George Wise, one of the founders of the village of Loomis.

The 1871 arrival of the railroad heading southeasterly toward Saginaw along the route approximately the same as followed by today's United States Highway US-10 accelerated the growth of Loomis, above. By 1887, with Seth Bowdish as postmaster, the 400 population town of Loomis boasted an extract factory, two shingle mills, a sawmill, along with a Methodist church and two hotels.

All that remains is a bar-restaurant and a defunct gasoline filling station store.

When Wise Township was organized in 1872, the first elections took place at the Loomis school house, left, electing Isaiah Windover as first township supervisor.

19th Century Village of Two Rivers (Caldwell) was a tourist spot.

Two Rivers (Caldwell), was a 19th Century play spot off Broomfield Road in Deerfield Township at a public access to the Chippewa River, originally called Caldwell after James C. Caldwell who moved from Fremont in 1882 to establish a hotel. The hotel was later the home of S.C. Smiley, who ran a store there, above right. A newer hotel was built by Will Richardson just east of the Smiley's store, *left*.

Transportation and roads improved, offering wider resort venues, leading to the hotel and the community's decline to today's cluster of residences.

Photos are from the turn of the 20th Century and come from postcards in the collection of the late Rosemary Reid.

Special Dedication
To Samuel W. Hopkins:

The man who gave Mt. Pleasant work.

"The commodious, modern and attractive home of Mr. and Mrs. Hopkins is a park-like place, the wide, spacious lawns being shady and inviting, ornamental and fruit trees, shrubbery, vines and flowers being in profusion, and because ten stately oaks grow near this beautiful residence the place is known as Oakten. It is on Normal Avenue and in the most desirable residential portion of the city. Here the many friends of the family often gather, finding an old-time hospitality and good cheer ever prevailing. The house is equipped with a splendid and carefully selected library, where Mr. Hopkins spends many pleasant hours, losing himself "in other men's minds," and is familiar with the world's best literature."

Isaac A. Fancher
Past and Present of Isabella County
1911

The above word picture of the home of Samuel Whalen and Margaretta Hopkins house was part of Fancher's nine page tribute to Hopkins in his book. The house was located at **630 South Normal Street, now University Avenue**, unfortunately, the best we can do to represent the man who probably is the single biggest factor in conversion from this sleepy lumber town in the middle of a swamp on a bluff overlooking the Chippewa River to a thriving manufacturing and educational center leading up to the dawn of the 20th Century. The last remnants of the house described, burned in an August, 1974 fire, 51 years after Hopkins 1923 death.

While no single individual can build a town and make it grow, the vision, ambition and leadership of Samuel W. Hopkins, *left in 1884*, was responsible for practically every major milestone in Mt. Pleasants commercial and educational history until the early 1920s.

It is appropriate the official release date of this book should be five days after the 120th Anniversary of the laying of the cornerstone of the first building on the original Central campus at Mt. Pleasant. But more about that later.

Samuel W. Hopkins was born in April, 1845, in Exeter, Rhode Island, the youngest of eight children of Judge Samuel and Freelove Burlingame Arnold Hopkins. He was a descendant of Declaration of Independence signer Stephen Hopkins. Learning came easy to Samuel W. and by age three he knew by heart Young's *First Reader* and Webster's *Spelling Book*, the two books he possessed. By eleven he could read and write, and by fourteen, with an invalid mother, two invalid sisters and a father with broken health, he was pretty much on his own while helping the others and striving for a higher education. In 1865, he graduated Fenton and Bigelow College in Cleveland, Ohio and began reading law with Benzeret H. Bill of Rockville, Ohio. In the fall of 1870, he entered the law department of the University of Michigan, graduating there in 1872, after which he visited his old home for awhile before returning to Michigan to locate in Grand Rapids, where he was admitted to the bar and did estate work that put him in central and northern Michigan.

While in Clare, he met Mt. Pleasant attorney/surveyor/businessman Isaac A. Fancher, who convinced him to come to Isabella County and join Fancher's legal practice. They were partners for three years. Hopkins then partnered with Michael Devereaux and Wade Smith for two years before partnering with a law school friend Free Estee. Hopkins was appointed Isabella County Clerk in 1873 and was then elected to three terms. He was justice of the peace for seven years. In 1874, he platted the Hopkins Addition to the City of Mt. Pleasant. He also served as Isabella County Prosecuting Attorney in 1875-76, then was elected to the Michigan Legislature in 1876 and re-elected in 1879, serving four years.

1892 was a busy year for Mr. Hopkins, he was elected to the Michigan Senate, he was chairman of the Mt. Pleasant Businessman's Association in charge of working to locate the United States Indian Industrial School in Isabella County. His correspondence with the area's district Congressman Bliss, secured the location for Mt. Pleasant.

That same year, he conceived of the idea of platting land and selling it to apply the proceeds to erecting a normal school here.

According to the Wikipedia online dictionary –"A **normal school** was a school created to train high school graduates to be teachers. Its purpose was to establish teaching standards or *norms*, hence its name. Most such schools are now called **teachers' colleges**; however, in some places, the term *normal school* is still used."

In the late 1800s, the teachers of Isabella County each year held a Teachers Institute at the county seat in Mt. Pleasant. During these institutes, tests would be given to high school graduates who wanted to become school teachers. If the person passed the tests, they were awarded a Teacher's Certificate. The number of one-room rural schools in the county, *ultimately to reach 115*, was growing and the demand for teachers was intense. Yet in 1882, the week-long summer institute was sparsely attended.

By 1890, there were an estimated 4,500 students regularly attending classes an average seven months per year, according to *The Enterprise* newspaper. These students were taught by 136 teachers, of which only three had teacher's certificates.

By 1892, the month-long summer normal had only 45 enrollees. The final test failure rate was so high that it was determined that the establishment of a formal normal school was needed. The year before only 10 out of 58 passed the teachers test.

M. K. Skinner, who had bought H. W. Jordan's Pen Art and Business College in 1891 planned to make improvements and add a full normal course, so people who wish to be teachers could earn a teachers certificate.

Samuel Hopkins, knowing 60 acres of the old Hursh farm at the south city limits were available, sketched a proposed sub-division, believing the sale of lots would make enough money to finance erection of a normal school building. He approached others with his plan.

Hopkins talked it over with friend, farmer and fellow member of the board of education Charles Brooks, who reacted favorably. The two shared the idea with John W. Hance, Michael Devereaux and

A. S. Cotant. That five then invited Wilkinson Doughty, George Dusenbury, Isaac A. Fancher, M. Lower, Douglas Nelson, F. D. Patterson, and L. N. Smith, to serve on a planning committee with them. The twelve formed the Mount Pleasant Improvement Company with a capital of $10,000 in shares of $25, which bought the 60 Hursh acres. Eight acres had already been subdivided, so company land consisted of 52 acres, with ten acres set aside for the college campus. The company sold 151 housing lots at a July 4, 1892, auction, for $110 each with the buyer asked to place $10 down and pay $10 per month for the second and third months and $5 per month on the balance until paid.

On September 13, 1892, the Central Michigan Normal School and Business Institute opened its doors on the second floor of the Carpenter Building at the southeast corner of Main and Michigan Streets. Five days later, the cornerstone was laid for the first building on the campus of what is now Central Michigan University. The Carpenter Building burned in the late 1990s.

Samuel W. Hopkins, *left in 1910*, later was President of the Mt. Pleasant Sugar Company and succeeded after years of effort to get the Michigan Condensed Milk Company to locate a plant in Mt. Pleasant at 300 West Broadway, later the Borden building, now Mt. Pleasant City Hall. Additionally, he was responsible for bringing a chicory processing plant to Mt. Pleasant.

Samuel and Margaretta Hopkins were married in 1873 had one son who died at one year old, and a daughter Lila Vedder, who married and moved to Gaylord, Michigan, then Detroit, with husband Jay Harris Buell.

While a member of the School Board, Hopkins took an active part in locating three sites for schools and erecting five school buildings. He worked with and made liberal contributions to the erection of the Isabella County Courthouse, the railroads, and the establishment of a Dow Chemical salt works at the north edge of Mt. Pleasant.

Margaretta Hopkins died in 1919 and Samuel W. Hopkins followed in 1923, having kept the towns commerce in steady growth and prepared for the oil boom that followed the discovery of the Mt. Pleasant oilfield in 1928, spurring the town's growth to new heights. Hopkins would have rejoiced.

Curiously, only a short street named after him is Mt. Pleasants sole tribute to Samuel W. Hopkins, scant reminder of the godfather of its growth.

jk

Why Do They Call It: Rosebush?

Travelers to Rosebush and Calkinsville from 1873 to 1889 or 1890 to 1903, went to the same place with both names. In 1868, James A. Bush platted a village around a store called Halfway in Isabella Township between Mount Pleasant and Clare. Bush gave land for a depot to the railroad if they would name it after his wife, Rose Bush. Elias B. Calkins got a post office in his store in 1873 and it was called Calkinsville. So freight and passengers went to Rosebush and mail to Calkinsville until 1889 when the post office name was changed to Rosebush. All was fine until 1890 when the post office name changed back to Calkinsville and in 1903 back to Rosebush, which stuck that time. *Above and below*, downtown Rosebush looking west from Mission Road in the 1920s and present day, respectively

A salute to Isabella County's black settlers.

No collection of Isabella County historical photos could be complete without salute our early black neighbors who joined the settling of the west side of our state and county. The black settlers, whose ancestors have organized as "The Old Settlers of Michigan", with the Chippewa Indians on the east side of the county and a variety of ethnicities and religious persuasions, made Isabella County a "poster child" for early diversity long before the term became a social and political football.

Typifying the "Old Settlers of Michigan" who settled in Isabella, Mecosta and Montcalm counties, the unknown woman, left, is symbolic of the African Americans who settled there in the 1860s from Ontario, Canada and Ohio after successfully escaping slavery via the Underground Railway. The first African American settlers under the Homestead Act of 1862 went into Rolland Township that year. In 1904, 60 Isabella County farms were African American owned.

Besides clearing land, homesteading and farming, many of the Old Settler's of Michigan African American men found work in the burgeoning lumber camps of Isabella County in the latter half of the 19th Century. A historical marker stands as part of a monument at Schoolsection Lake west of Remus in Mecosta County paying tribute to our areas black settlers. The Old Settlers, an organization of descendants of these black stalwarts, holds an annual reunion in August .

Oberlin School, below, built in 1920 at the southeast corner of Section 11, Rolland Township, Isabella County. In 1935, Oberlin School student body was, left to right: top row – Junior Jones, Duane Norman, Robert Hendricks, Junior Norman, Worthy Sawyer, Henry Nisonger, Leo Torpey; second row down – Jenny Morey, Francis Murray, Arlene Ward, Loraine Ward, teacher Velma Stout, Florence Murray, Vaneta Jones, Verna Taylor, Donna Jones, Olga Sagoff; third row down – Gerald Vebele, a second Junior Norman, Max Sawyer, Dean Taylor, Orville Hendricks; bottom row – Doris Morey, an unidentified Torpey, another unidentified Torpey, Donna Sawyer, Lois Taylor, Ione Sawyer and Betty Jones.

Isabella County Board of Supervisors at First Meeting of 1926.

At their first meeting of 1926, the Isabella County Board of Supervisors (forerunner of today's Isabella County Board of Commissioners) pose for their first formal picture as a group.
Left to right are:
Top Row – M. E. Brewer, C. N. Vance, Robert McGuire, Alvin Robart, Fred Nelson, Ira Walton, Charles Curtiss, M. F. Kenny and L. A. McGuire.
Bottom Row – E. L. Winslow, Floyd Bellows, Willis Genuine, Perry Thompson, Basil T. Pile, William Sellers, Christian Straus and John Watson.

Fritz School of Broomfield Township history defines multi-use: school; meeting hall; church; and now a bar.

Of the 115 one-room schools in Isabella County's past, none of the schoolhouses have had a more colorful history that the Fritz School at Coldwater Road and west M-20.

Organized in 1873 half-a-mile south of Broomfield Road on the east side of Coldwater Road, the Shank School lasted until 1901, when that school district disbanded, the school closed and it's fixtures and building were auctioned off. The district was then split between the District 8 Pony Creek School and the "new" District 5 Fritz School, where a building was built at the corner of Coldwater Roads at Michigan Highway M-20 in 1901.

FRITZ –1910. *Those who attended the Fritz School in 1910 with teacher* Anna Miller *(left) may or may not be included in this photograph, in no particular order, were:* Emma Heim, Ernest Leuder, Paul Leuder, Richard Leuder, Herman Leuder, Carl Leuder, August Fritz, Rudolf Fritz, Walter Maxon, Flora Maxon, Ethel Maxon, Mable Maxon, Roy Maxon, Thor Maxon, Ernest Leach, Daniel Leach, Charlie Ish, Lola Ish, Henery Ish, Emiel Rhode, Lester Hagerman, Lizzie Hagerman, Cecil Diehl, Howard Miller, Bernice Miller and Clayton Miller. Since the Fritz School closed in 1939, the building has had a colorful history. For awhile it was a Grange Hall

FRITZ – 1950s. Then the venerable old Fritz School became a temporary home for a Seventh Day Adventist congregation until a new building was erected in Mt. Pleasant in the 1960s. *Left to right in front of the church in 1950 are: front row –* Verlene Schedell, (?), (?), Josie Huston, Sharon Latham, Sharlene Denslow, Vere Craven, Harland Schedel, Robert Campbell, Robert Latham, David Dent; *second row –* Lawrence Wolcott *(teacher)* , (?), Veletta Craven, Vera Foster, Beverly Campbell, Bethy Huston, Viola Craven, (?), Veldy Craven, Vencil Craven.

FRITZ –2009 In 1978, Margurite Rice converted the building to the Barn Door Bar at the southeast corner of Coldwater Road and Michigan Highway M-20. Now owned by Mike and Cathy Pulverente, the Barn Door was Renovated but in this picture taken in early 2009, the door on the west end of the building, as well as three of the four windows on the south side of the building have remain unchanged, and the slight irregularity in the lower end of the dark wood above the door flags where the north wall of the old school was located. So now the room rings with "'nother round here" instead of the ABCs…. and raising two fingers means something altogether different.

Central Michigan University celebrated 120 years in 2012.

Central's first home. – On September 13, 1892, the Central Michigan Normal School and Business Institute opened its doors on the second floor of the Carpenter Building at the southeast corner of Main and Michigan Streets, shown above in the 1970s, upstairs over the Mt. Pleasant, later Smith's Drug Store. Michigan Historical Marker # L69C, was installed in 1968 at second floor level on the north side of the building facing Michigan Street reading: "Founded in 1892 as a private institution, Central Michigan Normal School and Business Institute held its first classes on this site. The institution became a state normal school in 1895. After several changes in name, the school became Central Michigan University."

The building burned in the late 1990s

With this vision fresh in his mind, Samuel Hopkins talked it over with friend, farmer and fellow member of the board of education Charles Brooks, who reacted favorably. The two shared the idea with John W. Hance, Michael Devereaux and A. S. Conant. That five then invited Wilkinson Doughty, George Dusenbury, Isaac A. Fancher, M. Lower, Douglas Nelson, F. D. Patterson, and L. N. Smith, to serve on a planning committee with them. The twelve formed the Mount Pleasant Improvement Company with a capital of $10,000 in shares of $25, which bought the 60 Hursh acres. Eight acres had already been subdivided, so company land consisted of 52 acres, with ten acres set aside for the college campus. The company sold 151 housing lots at a July 4, 1892 auction, for $110 each with the buyer asked to place $10 down and pay $10 per month for the second and third months and $5 per month on the balance until paid.

In private hands until 1895, Central Michigan Normal School and Business Institute became Central Michigan Normal School, a state institution, that year. The main administration building was augmented by a wing addition to the west in 1899, with another added to the west in 1902 to meet growing space needs of the robust young school.

At September 18, 1892, ceremonies the Central Michigan Normal School and Business Institute, officially broke ground for the school's first building on a ten acre plot south of town. On November 19, 1892, the cornerstone of the first building was laid in ceremonies conducted by the Knights of Pythias.

Central's 1912 Football Team.

The Central State Normal School football squad of 1912 poses at the edge of the athletic field behind Old Central Hall on the west side of the campus mall, approximately where Wightman Hall, on Washington Street now stands. In the background is the smokestack of the first campus power plant. While there are more people in the photo than the 1912 football team roster in the 1913 Central yearbook, those named, who played for Coaches Bruce Strickland and Harry Helmer are: Gerald Stilwell – Captain; Floyd Smith – Right Tackle; Leo Going – Left Tackle; Grover A. Buchan – Left Guard; Francis Campbell – Right Guard,; Ray Cheney – Left End; Frank Davidson – Left End; Ray Watkins – Left Halfback; Allen Graham – Right End; Dave Davidson – Left Tackle; Archie Leonard – Right Halfback; Russell Fraser – Fullback; and Marcel Lafromboise – Right End.

MT. PLEASANT MONTHLY MAGAZINE SEPTEMBER 2008

In 1956 the 2nd place winner of the Mt. Pleasant City-wide Christmas decorating contest religious category was the nativity scene-festooned front yard of the on-campus home of Central Michigan College President Charles Anspach. The house at 524 East Bellows Street, was built as a private residence in 1941 and purchased by Central in 1944 to be the home of Central's chief executive. The residence would be occupied by four Central presidents. Conversion of the house into an alumni center was complete in 1990. The restoration and expansion included the addition of a conference room, reception areas, staff offices, and workrooms, below. The modern

Central Michigan University Carlin Alumni House.

1957: Central Michigan College President Charles L. Anspach honored in print by CMC faculty on his birthday.

At 44 years old, Dr. Charles LeRoy Anspach became the fifth executive head of the school then known as Central Michigan College of Education in 1939, serving in that position until his 1959 retirement.

Anspach came from the automotive parts industry in his youth to be educated through his Masters of Arts level at Ashland College, now University, in Ohio and earned his doctorate at University of Michigan in 1930.

He was Registrar, then Dean of the College at Ashland through 1926, then became Head of the Education Department at Michigan State Normal College, Ypsilanti, Michigan (now Eastern Michigan University). In 1935 Dr. Anspach returned to Ashland as President of the College until 1939.

In a gentler time, long before the turbulent changes of the 1960s, the Central Michigan College faculty, in a rare move, honored Anspach in March, 1957, on the occasion of his 62nd birthday with a printed tribute, reproduced here.

He retired two years later, in 1959, and died in 1977.

Happy Birthday Prexy!
March 6, 1957

"The real worth of a man is not measured in terms of what people say of him nor by what people think of him. It is determined by the sum of his productive acts." Anon.

	1939	1956
Student Enrollment		
Undergraduate	1792	3404
Graduate	92	142
Off-Campus	400	2367
Total	2284	5913
Off-Campus Instruction		
Centers	5	45
Classes	55	180
Enrollment in courses	1063	5154
Physical Development		
Evaluation	$4,000,000	$24,000,000
Campus acreage	50	176
Volumes in Library	43,000	84,195
Vehicles	1	27
Telephones	50	215
Staff		
Faculty	111	258
Doctors degrees	17	78
Office staff	9	55
Service staff	35	145
Degrees Granted	255	538
Students Housed		
Residence hall beds	278	2150
Married students in apartments	0	283

New Programs and Expansion
- Bachelor of Music Degree established in 1946
- Division of Clinical Services started in 1946
- Interstate Intercollegiate Athletic Conference 1950
- Bachelor of Science in Business Administration authorized in 1951
- Reserve Officers Training Corps established in 1952
- Placed on the approved list of A.A.U.W. in 1952
- Masters Degree Program 1954

Grants for Research and Special Studies
- Fund for Advancement of Education 1952 —
- Atomic Energy Commission 1955, 1956, 1957
- Dow Chemical Company 1955

Budget		
State	$320,000	$3,032,000
Local	44,000	286,000
Self-Liquidating	12,500	1,027,000
Public Services	30,000	290,000
Total	$406,500	$4,635,000
Salary Schedule		
Instructor to Professor	$1800 - 4000	$4800 - 9000
Miscellaneous		
Student and Faculty automobiles registered	0	2028
Married students	0 (?)	773
Veterans (approximately 1000 at peak)		556

The men of the faculty at Central Michigan College take this means of expressing their appreciation to President Charles L. Anspach for his dynamic leadership which has stimulated the tremendous growth of Central Michigan College over the past eighteen years.

Center grounds await future disposition for "new beginning."

The Mt. Pleasant Center, in the northwest corner of the City of Mt. Pleasant, which closed in October, 2009, and remains in a "much-rumored, but no concrete announced plan" limbo. The core of the facility was established as an Indian Industrial School in the latter decade of the 19th century

The 1890-91 session of the United States Congress saw Congressman Aaron T. Bliss of Saginaw *(later to be governor of Michigan)* gain passage of a bill providing for the establishment and construction of Indian industrial schools in Wisconsin, Michigan, and Minnesota designed after the plan of the Indian school in Carlise, Pennsylvania. The bill further stipulated that the buildings for the state of Michigan should be in the county of Isabella *(see plaque on the former main building, right)*. In his 1911 book, *Past and Present of Isabella County*, Isaac Fancher says, *"The people of Isabella County, and especially the Indians, feel very grateful for the efforts of Congressman Bliss in securing this school, for without the appropriation (of funds to secure the grounds for the Isabella County school) we could not have hoped to locate one here."* The U.S. Department of the Interior purchased the east half of Section 9, Union Township, in the northwest corner of Mount Pleasant bounded by Crawford, River, Bamber, and Pickard roads.

Fancher continues his 1911 narrative about the school: *"Their outfit of buildings at the present time consists of seven brick buildings are: one two story building with basement and attic fully utilized; an assembly building; a girls dormitory; a boys dormitory; a building for a dining room, domestic science and bakery; a hospital building; a power house; a laundry; a storehouse; an industrial building that includes a blacksmith shop, tailor and shoe shop, and a carpenter shop (all used for preparing students for employment). There are several wooden buildings including a barn, storing building; three cottages for employees; a piggery; a farm barn; and a farm house.*

"There are over 300 students at the school. Quite a number of them have graduated and are in the government employ.

"Knowing the tribal life of the Indian, one is surprised to see how soon they change to a large extent from their roving life to one of industry and good husbandry (farming). In their school all the common branches are taught, besides which they have domestic science and manual training. Many of them have good voices and are quite proficient in music. The school supports a good brass band and they play baseball and football with proficiency.

"One thing the authorities of the school are to be complimented for is the preservation of the forty acres of native forest situated just north of the plat on which the buildings are located."

Those forty acres of forest has been preserved to modern times.

The Mt. Pleasant Indian Industrial School operated until 1934, when the land was turned over to the state of Michigan, which converted its use to the Mt. Pleasant branch of the Michigan Home and Training Schools, institutions for the mentally challenged.

The hospital on the grounds continued to function as Mt. Pleasant's hospital *(below)* until the Central Michigan Community Hospital was completed on Brown Street in 1946.

This aerial view from the south of the Mt. Pleasant Industrial School shows the complex of buildings comprising the hub of the school's activities. For orientation purpose, Crawford Road *(Harris Street extension north of the City Limit)* is just beyond the right border.

Reports of the Mt. Pleasant Industrial School experience vary from discontent to gratitude for a steady environment with regular meals, board, and vocational training. In 1938, more than 600 Chippewa alumni of the school held a powwow there to celebrate their years at the school.

In October, 2009, now named the Mt. Pleasant Center, the institution was closed as the recession continues and the state seeks to tighten purse strings.

The fate of the grounds and facilities *(awaiting a new beginning)*, now the property of the City of Mt. Pleasant is uncertain at this writing.

The former Indian Industrial School grounds, left, is shown during 1956 Mt. Pleasant Home and Training School facilities expansion, grew rapidly during the 1970s. For older-timers, that's the Leonard Refinery on West Pickard at the top, slightly right of center, with Ferro Stamping Company (now the Commerce Building), the current home of *The Morning Sun* newspaper, in the upper right corner.

MID-MICHIGAN HISTORY   Jack R. Westbrook

THE MORNING SUN –AUGUST 18, and SEPTEMBER 16, 2010
Island Park: Long the center of Mt. Pleasant leisure activities.

Before the business expansion of Mission Street and residential growth of other areas of town decentralized Mt. Pleasant lifestyles, Island Park was the year-round center of sports, recreational and social life.

Left, in the ariel photo from the 1940s, note the rooftop swimming pool (partial oval at middle left edge); tennis courts just right of the swimming pool; the millpond, upper left; Harris Mill along Broadway in the upper left quadrant and the grandstand and race track at the center.

Right, looking north at Island Park from just behind the Borden Building on Broadway, there the Mt. Pleasant Swimming Pool on the right and the back of the grandstand on the left.

Left, in 1985, the now-closed swimming pool is shown during one of the last of many annual Chippewa River spring floods the venerable structure had endured before having it's life cut short stealthily with the stroke of a government budgeter's pen.

Viewed from Broadway Street looking north, the flooded tennis courts and utility building representing all that remained of the razed grandstand are shown equally awash.

The Mt. Pleasant Municipal Swimming Pool was built about 1938 in the southeast segment of Island Park, offering rooftop swimming, locker rooms and showers. Girls made a left circuit of the ground floor while boys made a right, to wade a shallow foot-cleansing pool and climb the steps to the pool.. That's the back of the Isaac Fancher house, at Main Street and Chippewa Street, peeking through the trees in the background.

Raucous laughter in Island Park in summer came from the rooftop of the elegantly designed Mt. Pleasant Municipal Swimming Pool where everybody who was anybody in kidland (not out, briefly on vacation) came to splash and socialize.

In those days when travel was a rare treat, entire summers would be a delightful string of days spent "at the pool".

August is traditional Isabella County Fair Month.

Since the 1880s, the second Saturday in August has hallmarked the opening of the week-long Isabella County Youth and Farm Fair. For the first several years, the Fair was held just north of Mt. Pleasant along the Chippewa River on grounds just north of the curve where North Fancher Avenue turns into Industrial Avenue ... behind the present-day offices of Lease Management, Inc.

In 1899, the Isabella County Fair Board sold it's property north of town to Dow Chemical Company, who built a plant there which operated for a short time.

With the proceeds of that sale, the Fair Board enhanced the former Fancher's Meadows property and made an agreement to hold the Fair there annually at the place we know as Island Park in Mt. Pleasant *(photos above and below)*.

For decades during Fair Week, downtown Mt. Pleasant was live with the hurly-burly of carnival music; echoing with squeals of midway riders and assorted whinnies, moos, clucks, and oinks of non-human fairgoers; the aroma of cotton candy and the aforementioned non-human participants; and the blaring sounds of whatever performances were appearing in front of the grandstand. North Main Street became a daily traffic snarl (only partially recreated by last month's Summerfest).

Finally outgrowing Island Park, the Isabella County Youth and Farm Fair (in 2009 enlivened by activities related to this year's Isabella County 1859-2009 Sesquicentennial celebration) acquired grounds on Mission Road and located north of town again in 1978.

Former Mt. Pleasant Indian Industrial School/Mt. Pleasant Island Park Ice Skating Rink lent hometown warmth to winter.

Many a young Mt. Pleasant romance began on the ice of the Island Park free ice skating rink which was supervised by the City of Mt. Pleasant. A warming house at the base of the grandstand provided hot chocolate for sale. The ice rink was "the place to be" for generations of Mt. Pleasant kids until it's discontinuation in the 1980s. On quiet winter evenings, it is said longtime Mt. Pleasant residents still hear echoes of the laughter and muted blare of piped-in music that hallmarked the frosty long ago nights at Island Park's ice skating rink. Right, Mt. Pleasant city employees flood the area in front of the grandstand as soon as the weather got cold enough to form an ice rink.

H. Edward Deuel Bridge honors Mayor who bought Island Park.

Serving as the main entrance to Mt. Pleasant's Island Park from the downhill west end of L1ncoln Street at North Main Street, the bridge is named for H. Edward Deuel, the 11th – 1903-05, 15th – 1909-10, 17th – 1912, and 19th – 1914-1915 Mayor of the City of Mt. Pleasant. The flatland known alternately as Fancher's Meadows, Fancher's Flats and Fancher's Grove, served by the wooden bridge shown above in 1906, was purchased by the City in 1909. A canal was dug at the west side of the newly acquired lands and Island Park was born. The wooden bridge was replaced by a cement span bridge and was moved to the southwest corner of the park and became known as the Oak Street Bridge. Deuel pushed for a grandstand and racetrack for the new park and persuaded the Isabella County Fair to move there, where the annual Fair took place for decades.

New Cement Bridge over Chippewa River on Broadway offers new avenues to the West Side of Mt. Pleasant.

The West Broadway Bridge over the Chippewa River – Following the 1910 collapse of a wooden bridge spanning the Chippewa River just west of the Ann Arbor depot on West Broadway, a new cement bridge was constructed, *above*. When it was built, Mt. Pleasant was able to boast having the longest cement span bridge in Michigan. The title didn't last long, but enthusiatic Mt. Pleasant boosters snapped up "Longest Span" post cards, origin of the above scene, as soon as they were printed to send to potenial newcomers. In 2010, refurbished, reinforced and repainted many times, the bridge continues to serve, but with the clop-clop of horse traffic replaced by the whisper of automobile tires.

Nagy's Power-Flight Service was a West Broadway fixture.

You pulled up to the gas pump, triggering a "ding" as you ran over the air hose stretched across the driveway, then *rolled down* your car window as the attendant came out to greet you. "Can I help you?" he asks. "Fill 'er up", you said "and while you're at it, could you check the oil and maybe the radiator … car's been running a little hot lately." "Yessir", came the reply "and maybe I should look at the tire pressure. This left rear looks a little low." The scenario may sound strange to those raised in this "self-serve and pick up a quart of milk" world of multui-function "convenience stores with gas pumps" era but was commonplace not so long ago. One example of such service stations was Nagy's Refinery Service at 1001 West Broadway, on the southwest corner of Broadway and Harris streets on Mt. Pleasant's west side. Mike "Milo" Nagy owned and operated the business from the mid-1950s until his retirement in 1968. The building has served a variety of businesses and was for a time a private residence. Since the Nagy era, it has been Lynn Jones gasoline and service station, Jack West's Used Car Sales and most recently the home of J & B Used Cars. Nagy perished in a boating accident at Brimley in Michigan's Upper Peninsula May 1, 1986. While personal service with your gasoline fill-up has gone the way of fifty cent a gallon gasoline (pump on the left in this photo reads thirty-two cents per gallon) and "Can I help you?" is a long forgotten phrase on the gasoline pump apron, the spirit of the corner automotive repair service embodied by Nagy and his ilk lives on in rare places today.

Springtime in Mt. Pleasant. Did you bring your waders?

The arrival of spring and snowmelt in days gone by raised havoc with Mt. Pleasant life and transport. Top right, Bill Nye stands in his flooded front yard at his south end Mt. Pleasant home March 17, 1919. Top left, a 1930s driver splashes along the 200 block of Chippewa Street just north of the Isabella County Jail. Out on Mission Street (then U. S. Highway 27) ten years later, below left, a damp parade traverses "Lake Mission" in the 800 block, just south of the High and Mission Street intersection. The south Mission flooding problem in spring, and any other heavy rain time, persisted until the 1970s. Island Park, below, was also a perennial target for the overflowing Chippewa River usually in the springtime, a condition that continues to the present. Note the cupolas on atop the Borden Building, upper right, looking as bold and architecturally distinct as those reconstructed as part of the present West

Broadway Restoration artisan/workers have made their modern cupola counterparts. Peeking through the trees just left center above the Mt. Pleasant Municipal Swimming Pool (a victim of "bulldozer restoration" rather than floods) is the top of the feed milling company, Bader's, incinerated as a drill for the Mt. Pleasant Fire Department in the late 1960.

Bader Milling Company later moved to the Borden Building.

Magnificent Comeback: The Borden Building to City Hall.

The dowager queen of Mt. Pleasant historic buildings is newly bejeweled and returned to her throne. This crowning glory of all Mt. Pleasant new beginnings culminated near the end of 2008 with the formal dedication of the new City of Mt. Pleasant offices in the restored Borden Building at 320 West Broadway, after many years and attempts to return the building to its rightful place as a centerpiece for Mt. Pleasant's icons.

The Broadway Street-level shot below show the Borden Building, built in 1907, at work processing milk from more than 2,000 area cows weekly and was closed in 1960.

Through the years many attempts to find a use for the building failed until the unique parternship of city and state government with private enterprise saw the Mt. Pleasant City Commission take a stand with the West Broadway Revitalization project over the protests of nay-sayers who fretted about tax impact.

Not only did the city see the worthwhile preservation project through …. but announced December 8, 2008 that 2009 city taxes would be lowered, earning a huge "attaboy" from history mavens and taxpayers alike.

A look at early 20th century Isabella County life through the journal of resident Glenn Stacy.

Toward the middle of the second decade of 21st century in a world where in some camps crisis is defines as "having only two bars on my cellphone" and "what do you mean this is not a wi-fi hotspot?", it is always interesting to look at the world of what Tom Brokaw called "the greatest generation". Now it looks like, after more than 50 years of growth and prosperity, we are facing long and narrow financial straits and perhaps a curtailment of the lifestyle that a half-century of priviledge brought. For some tighter times will be like Yogi Berra's "déjà vu all over again".

One of those veterans of the Great Depression (1929-1940) and World War II is Glenn Stacy of East Blanchard Road in Lincoln Township. Last month I spent some time with the vital and outspoken 94-year old Glenn and was able to get a copy of his "work-in-progress" journal being written by he and his wife Donna Lee Chivington-Stacy and transcribed by their daughter-in-law Joyce Stacy. My thanks to the Stacy family for allowing me to share this tale with the MPMM readership audience.

Glenn Stacy with a photo of himself and Army buddies in Egypt.

The following is a slightly edited version of the early portions of that journal:

I, Glenn Stacy, was born March 15, 1915 at my grandparents (Stacy) farm on Wing Road in Union Township, Isabella County, Michigan. The doctor in attendence was Dr. Powers of Dushville, now Winn. My grandparents on my father's side were Mary Ann Nitz (1852-1920) and John Newton Stacy (1843-1922). My grandparents on my mother's side were Lucinda Jane Wooton (1867-1944) and Daniel Gabriel Niswonger (1864-1959), My parents were Allen Maynard Stacy and Nettie Adona Stacy.

Soon after my birth, my grandparents moved to Pine Street in Mt. Pleasant and my parents remained on the farm where I grew up along with my sister Edith (1919), twins Hazel and Helen (1921) and baby brother Daniel (1923). We were small farmers on 65 acres with 6 cows, some chickens and pigs. We grew a large garden, from which my mother canned about 600 quarts of fruit and vegetables each year and would take eggs to town on Saturday to trade them for groceries.

Farmers traveled little in the early days so I only got to town a couple times each year.

DECORATION (now Memorial) DAY –*My grandfather Stacy was a Civil War Veteran and Decoration Day was a big deal in Mt. Pleasant and we would go to see the parade where there was a band, a procession of veterans and many speeches at the Isabella County courthouse grounds.*

FOURTH OF JULY – *Again a day of parades, a band concert on the courthouse grounds and fireworks at night. My uncle Harley, my dad's brother, had a party store on the west side of North Main Street across from the courthouse. He had a soda bar and when we went to town on the occasions listed above, dad would take us to*

The Stacy kids on the farm at Whiteville and Wing Roads in 1923. Left to right – Glenn Jay, Daniel, Edith and twins Helen and Hazel.

Harley and Mabel Stacy, proprietors, at the left, pose with other Stacy's in front of Stacy's Variety Store at 117 North Main Street (west side of the street). The store operated only a short time in the late 1920s just into the 1930s, when Harley died.

Uncle Harley's store for an ice cream cone.
Uncle Harley married the former Mabel Coomer. Her father owned a farm on Wing Road and he donated land to the Methodist Church group for what is now the Coomer Methodist Church. My father was of the Methodist faith and, although my mother was Baptist she decided we should be baptized when I was about ten years old. So all us kids: Edith; Hazel; Helen; Daniel and myself were baptized one Sunday at the Coomer Church. Grandad Stacy was with the Ohio National Guard as his home was in Bowling Green, south of Toledo. They came to Michigan when my dad was about four years old because of much cheaper land. They cut maple logs and had lumber made to build their barn and enlarge the house on the Wing Road farm. After my grandma Stacy died, Grandpa Stacy came to live with us on the farm when I was about seven years old. I enjoyed him telling me things about the Civil War. I wish I had been older when he told me those stories and could remember more. But one thing I know is that there was a lot of sorrow, death, and folks made cripples for life in that terrible war.
SCHOOL – Maple Hill School was about a mile and three-quarters from home so mom home-taught me until I was about seven years old. I was bright enough when I started school that I made two grades in one year and so caught up to the rest of the class that had started before me.
During summer vacation when I was both seven and then eight I spent two weeks at my grandparents (Niswonger) on North Shepherd Road in Chippewa Township. My grand dad would take my cousin Anna Jane and myself fishing in the Chippewa River. He had a big old wood boat and would pole it up

stream with a 12 foot pole. Then we would drift down, fishing along the way. That night we would clean the fish we caught, soak them in salt water and fry them the next morning.

I graduated eighth grade in the spring of 1929 and that fall stayed in Mt. Pleasant with my Aunt Alice and Uncle John Dangler so that I could attend 9th grade at the Central Michigan College Training School. In the fall of 1930 my mother had a serious operation and my dad was working evenings at the sugar refinery so I lived at home to help do chores and cook for my family. I rode to school that fall with Stuart Merrill and had to walked about a mile and a half each morning to their plac and then walk about four miles each night home from where Merrills farmed.

Mt. Pleasant was an oil town and so never felt the Great Depression of 1929-1940. I was a poor country boy and so I felt lucky. I did so well in high school, getting good grades, being in the Senior play and earning a track letter. I graduated high school in 1933.

It was during the Depression so I had no money to go to college. The winter of 1933-34 I stayed with a cousin, Walter Stacy, in Lansing trying to get a job in the Oldsmobile Auto factory where he and another cousin worked. My home was out of the "Hiring zone" (30 mile radius from Lansing) so I was unable to get work there. I came home and worked on the farm for my Uncle Walter Niswonger for $5.00 a week and room and board (all I could eat ... Aunt Stella was a fine cook!!!).

I took a business correspondence course with the American Technical Society in Chicago. It was a two year course in bookkeeping, business management, inventory and salesmanship. I graduated in 1934 .

I applied for work at the Borden milk condensery plant in Mt. Pleasant and they forwarded my letter of application to their Division office at LaSalle Street in Chicago, just a few blocks from the offices of American Technical Institute so Borden's Division Manager checked out my record with the school.

When he found out my grades, wired the Mt. Pleasant plant to hire me as soon as possible. That's how I got a job in November 1934 making thirty cents an hour.

Glenn Stacy worked for Bordens until joining the Army after the attack on Pearl Harbor. After World War II (but that's another story for later) Stacy returned to Bordens as Office Manager in 1945, then was Assistant Cashier for Exchange Savings Bank from 1947 until 1951, when he returned to Bordens as office manager. The Borden plant closed in 1960 and Glenn Stacy went to Central Michigan College in the Stores and Purchasing department, from which he retired in 1982 as Senior Purchasing Agent.

Chickory Plant an early 20th Century Mt. Pleasant employer.

201 East Pickard Street was the site of a plant operating from the late 1910s to late 1930s to process the chickory abundant in mid-Michigan. Chicory is a homeopathic medicine sometimes used as a coffee substituite. The plant closed in the 1930s.

In 2010 (left) the site is the home of the ReStore, which accepts donations of all sorts of merchandise and building materials, resold to the public to benefit Habitat for Humanity.

THE MORNING SUN –OCTOBER 29, 2010

Sugar Beet Plant sweetened the Mt. Pleasant job market in 1930s.

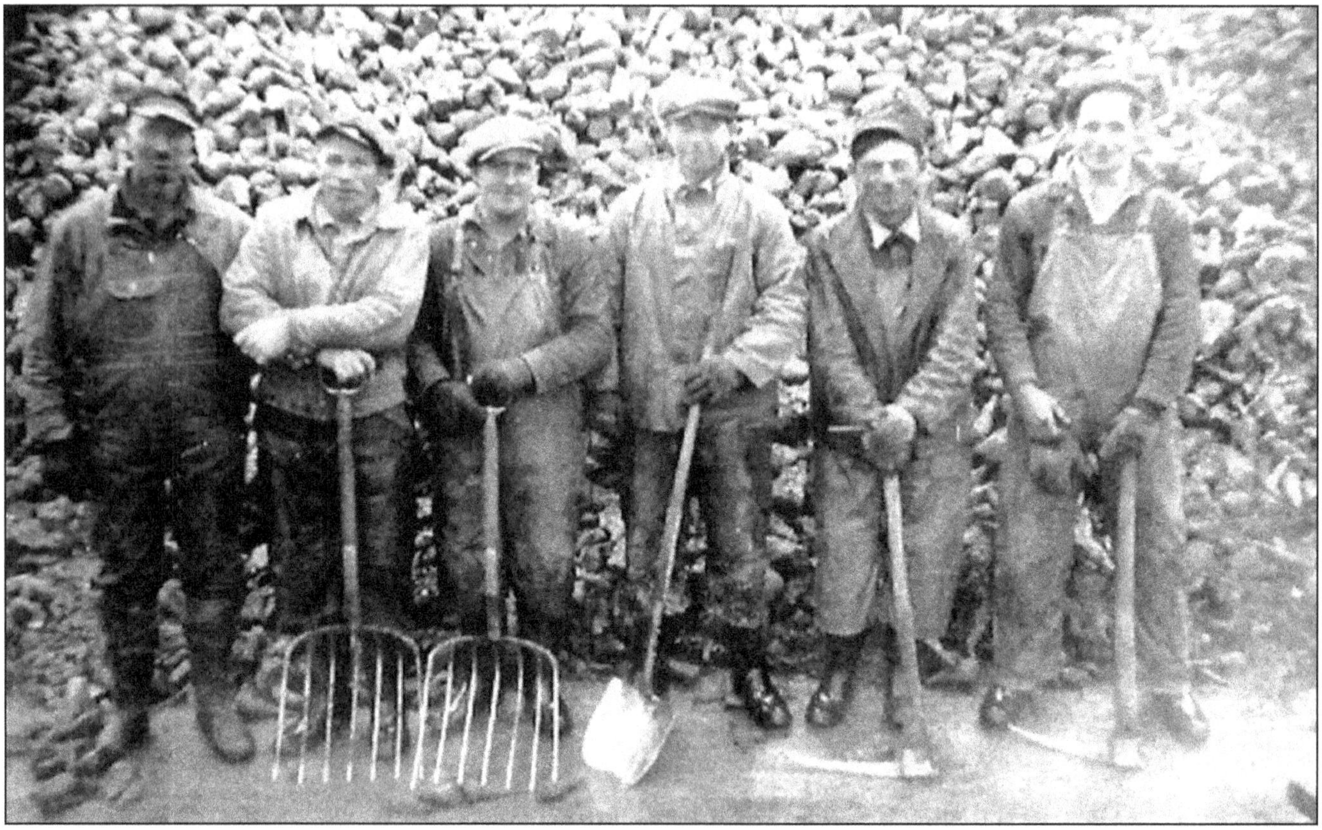

210 West Pickard – During the Great Depression, the Mt. Pleasant sugar beet processing plant was running three shifts and was welcome employment, albeit seasonal. The second shift at the Michigan Sugar Mt. Pleasant plant, in this undated 1930s photo, above, included: Lawrence Recker, Clarence Feltman, Marvin Hake, Ross Lindy, H. C. Walderf and Chester Davis. The plant produced an average of 233,000 bags of sugar in the seven years from 1935 to 1942.

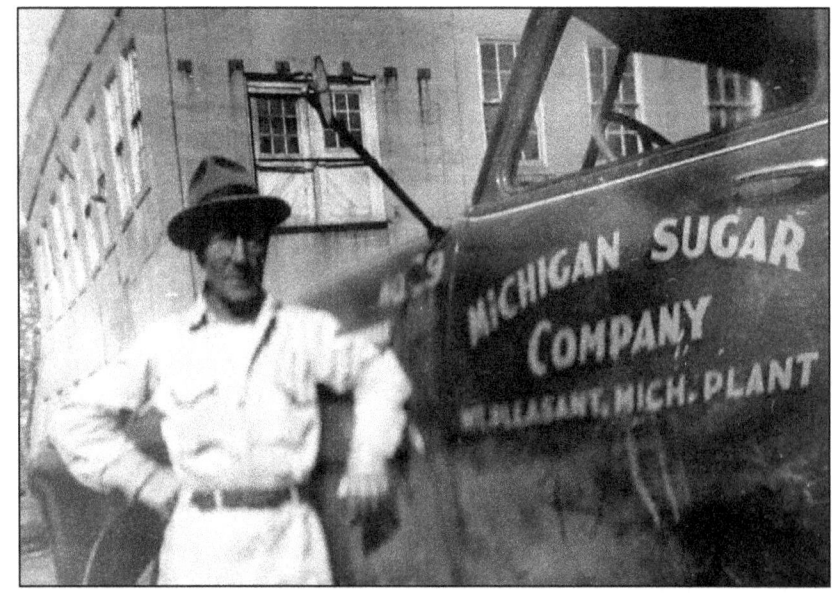

Left, Howard Sweet worked as a driver for the company after having been employed for several years by Renwick Elevator (later Bader Milling) downtown, where the city parking lot facing Broadway in front of Riverside Apartment Towers is now located.

Dow Chemical 1903-1930 Mt. Pleasant presence.

![Dow Chemical Co. Mt. Pleasant, Mich.]

From 1903 until 1930, Dow Chemical Company operated a salt works at the very north end of Fancher Street with the plant on the south side of the Chippewa River, above, and property to the north of the river dotted with brine wells. The property had been purchased from the Isabella County Fair Board and was the site of the county's first fairs, north of the present Lease Management Inc. at the Fancher/Industrial streets corner. When the salt works closed in 1930, Dow deeded their property north of the river to the Mt. Pleasant Country Club and the land facing Mission Street became Lee Equipment Company. Below, the site of Indian Mills/Isabella City, Mt. Pleasants "seedling" settlement, is seen at the bridge, right, from the tower of the salt works.

The Clarke Historical Library in the Park Library Building on the Mt. Pleasant campus of Central Michigan University featured an exhibit called "Drilling for Brine: The Dow Chemical Plant on Mt. Pleasant 1903-1930" through the summer of 2013.

Mt. Pleasant Country Club; an eight decade activity center.

The Mt. Pleasant Country Club, *above* in a 1935, aerial photo, celebrated its 81st birthday in 2012. The club was formed in 1921 as a loosely organized group who played golf on property about where the Citgo gasoline filling station sits today on West Pickard Street at "golf links located east of Harris Street and north of Pickard Street" according to a May 26, 1921 story in the *Mt. Pleasant Times*. The first president was R. A. Cochman, Superintendent of the Mt. Pleasant Indian Industrial School. The next year, the club had to vacate that property and began looking for a new home. In 1922, now 50 members strong and named the Mt. Pleasant Country Club, the group acquired 70 acres from Dow Chemical Company on the north side of the Chippewa River from the former Dow Chemical Salt Works on Mission Road.

In 1927, the Club built the first rudimentary clubhouse, then built a larger one in 1934, aided by an influx of new members from the bustling oil and gas exploration and production industry shielding the town from the financial devastation suffered by most of the country during the (1929-1939) Great Depression. A screened porch, absent in the above photo, was built in 1937. Beginning in 1949, the Country Club began hosting the Annual Michigan Oil And Gas Association Picnic/Reunion the third Thursday of each June, a tradition that continues. The clubhouse pictured above burned in 1985 and was replaced by a modern structure.

Valley Chemical Company.

Alongside the Chippewa River downstream from Mt. Pleasant between Mission and Isabella roads on East Valley Road northeast of town about three miles, Valley Chemical Company, shown here in the mid-1950s, operated from 1928 until 1964. Valley Chemical was a rendering plant, converting animal carcasses and commercial waste fats into other useful chemicals. None of the buildings remain on the site, razed to make room for a new highway route, now intersected by the U.S. 127 freeway.

What The Heck Is It? ….. and who was Smith Manufacturing ?

Recently Mt. Pleasant's John McDonald knocked on my door with the object below in hand, along with the question "Have you ever heard of Smith Manufacturing in Mt. Pleasant?" followed by "What is it?"

The whatcha-ma-call-it has "Smith Manufacturing" stamped on the reverse side.

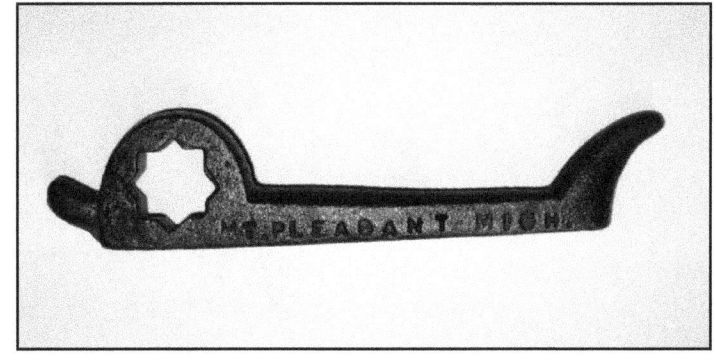

It looks like it could be a key ….. the counter/guide for a printing press … some kind of wrench …. or….. you name it.

Even if named, the question of who was the mysteries Smith Manufacturing, where were they and when.

If you know the answer to any or all of the perplexities, call (989) 773-5741.

HE MORNING SUN – AUGUST 12, 2010

Pere Marquette arrives at Mt. Pleasant in 1879.

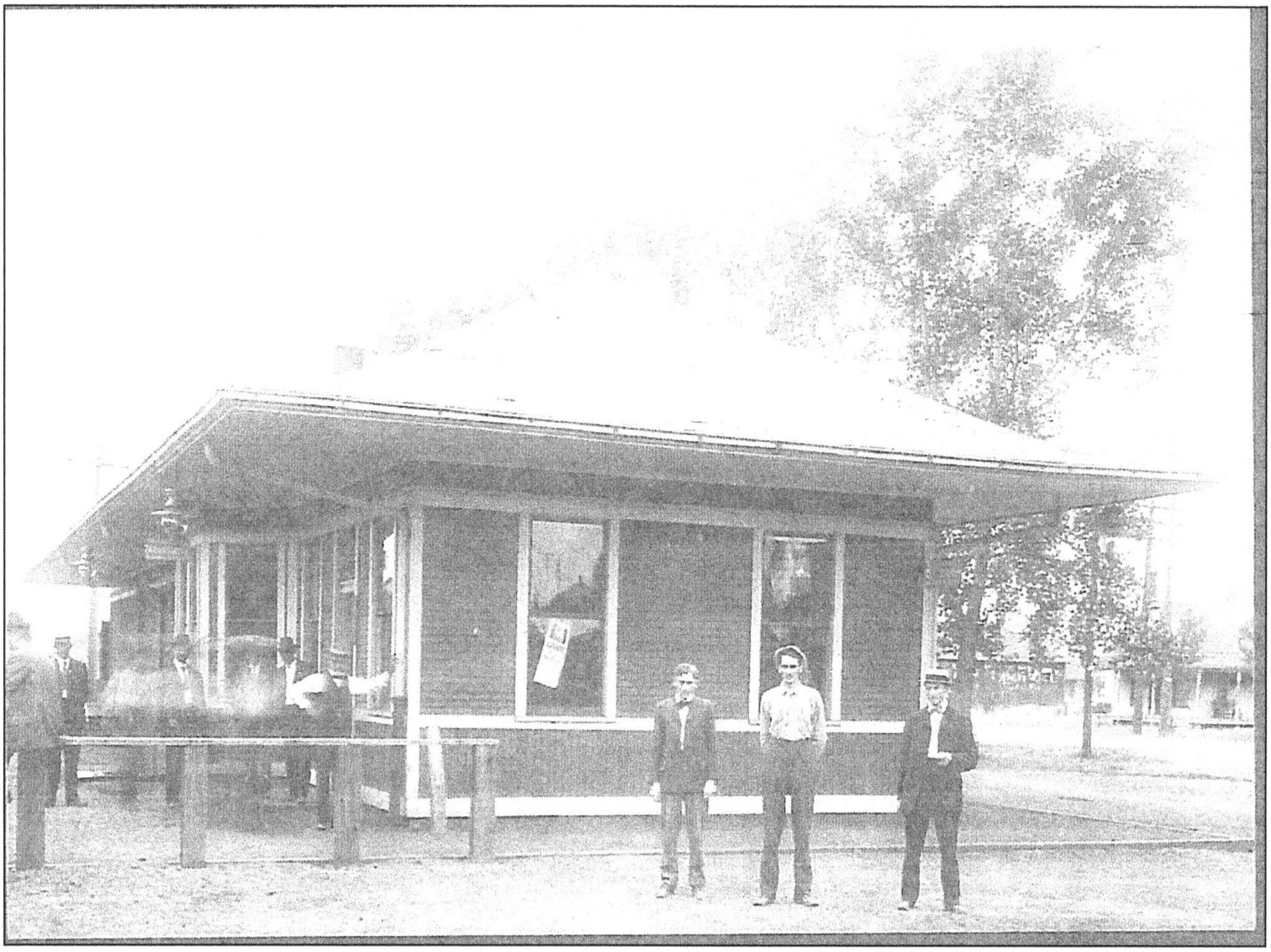

625 North Main Street – The first Mt. Pleasant railroad depot was built on this location in 1879 for a narrow guage Pere Marquette train track linking the town with Coleman.

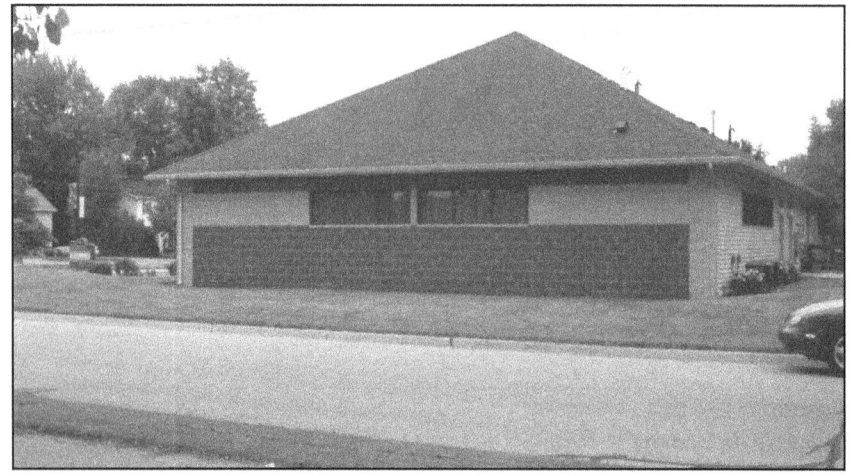

Following a 1930s fire, the building was sold and moved to to 215 Palmer Street. The man in the center above is Frank Brownson. A replacement building was later razed and a new office building built in the late 1980s. The present building houses the offices of the Michigan Education Association and Whitford Chiropractic.

Why are Mt. Pleasant High School teams called "The Oilers"?

The Laura Root #1 oil well, discovery well of the Mt. Pleasant oil field, was almost astraddle the Isabella/Midland county line. Being located almost equal distance from Mt. Pleasant and Midland, either could have become the place to live, commute to the field.

When the Mt. Pleasant field discovery well was reportedly looking good in mid 1928, Walter Russell sprung into action, spearheading a group of Mt. Pleasant businessmen who pratically overnight leased pipeline right-of-way from the discovery well to the railhead at Mt. Pleasant, securing an easy route to market for the crude oil from that field, when the discovery well came in August 29, 1928.

The oil, the equipment suppliers, the people and the resultant cashflow, went to Mt. Pleasant instead of Midland, just ahead of the Great Depression. Mt. Pleasant became the Oil Capital of Michigan,

Because the presence of an active oil and natural gas exploration and production industry presences, Mt. Pleasant felt little of the Depression's financial chaos. In appreciation for the oil industry's role in Mt. Pleasant's comparative prosperity during the Great Depression, the name of Mt. Pleasant High School athletic teams was changed to the "Oilers".

Mt. Pleasant Hosts 25,000 visitors to Oil Exposition in 1935.

Central State Teachers College's Doctor Joseph Carey, of the Mount Pleasant Planning Commission and Chamber of Commerce President N. G. "Harry" Gover hold a sign for the 1935 Michigan Oil and Gas Exposition, which drew more than 25,000 people to town.

A parade led by a mock hearse containing an effigy of "Ole Man Depression" symbolizing industry activity having shielded the area from the financial devastation of the Great Depression.

So great were the crowds at the Exposition that overnight a pedestrian bridge was fabricated at bottom of the hill, below, at the Main Street entrance to the park to avoid vehicle-people mishaps. Note the welder working into the first night of the expo to complete the bridge, left, which was in use well into the 1970s as a pedestrian overpass and "kids on bikes thrill ride".

Michigan oil and gas industry picnic/reunions a third Thursday of June Mt. Pleasant tradition at Country Club.

In 1934 the Michigan Oil And Gas Asociation (MOGA), an organization of Michigan oil and gas explorationists/producer (and supportive supply and service firms) was officially chartered in Mt. Pleasant. The group organized primarily to combat wellhead price disparities but ultimately to foster a legislative environment conducive to the orderly development of Michigan oil and natural gas resources.

Semi-annual banquet gathering for MOGA directors began in the summer of 1934 at Mt. Pleasant. One of the first, left, had the first MOGA President Howard Atha, seated at the head table with Harold McClure Sr., MOGA Executive Secretary A. G. Weidman and Michigan Chief State Geologist Dr. R. A. Smith.

From 1934 to 1938, semi-annual banquets were held, the mid-year gathering taking place at Mt. Pleasant. In 1939, the first official MOGA Summer Picnic open to the general membership took place at the Alma home of then MOGA President Harold Mc Clure Sr.. At right below, Michigan Governor M. D. Van Wagoner arrives at a summer outing accompanied by Mt. Pleasant's Walter Russell (who leased pipeline right of way from Pure Oil's Mt. Pleasant Field discovery well at the Midland-Isabella County border in 1928 to the wellhead in Mt. Pleasant, assuring a market-route for oil from that field and establishing Mt. Pleasant as the oil capital of Michigan), greeted by McClure.

The 1941-1945 World War II years saw limited summer outings (none in 1943 and 1945) in various parts of the state. In 1946 until the present, the MOGA Annual Picnic/Reunion has been held at the Mt. Pleasant Country Club, shown below left in the early 1980s. Below right, Longtime MOGA Picnic Co-chairmen Muskegon Development's William Myler, MOGA President Frank L. Mortl, and MOGA Picnic Co-chairman Lease Management's Jack Harkins greeted MOGA Picnic Michigan oilpatch newcomers and veterans from the state, nation and world for many years.

MID-MICHIGAN HISTORY   Jack R. Westbrook

T. PLEASANT MONTHLY MAGAZINE – JULY, 2009

Norman X. Lyon: oil and gas editor; Kiwanian; Mayor.

"Lyon known for writings on oil, service to community" read the front page headline of the September 30, 1991 Mt. Pleasant *Morning Sun*, reporting the death, at 84, of the man whose reporting put Michigan and Mt. Pleasant "on the map" as an important oil and natural gas producing province, as well as distinguishing himself as an outstanding community citizen.

Norman X. Lyon was born in 1907 in Leonadis, Michigan and, after 1929 graduation from Albion College, worked briefly for the Greenville (MI) *Daily News*. The following spring, a friend told him of temporary opening as editor of the Mt. Pleasant *Times-News*. "I came to Mt. Pleasant to fill in at the paper for three months and never left" he liked to quip.

In 1933 he was a charter member of the Mt. Pleasant Kiwanis Club, where he remained active until his final 1991 illness. He was also an avid sportsman, enjoying hunting and fishing as a longtime member of the Pere Marquette Hunting and Fishing Club, one of Michigan's oldest such group.

The Mt. Pleasant oil field, discovered in 1928, drew an influx of people, jobs and, through both capital expenditures and royalties to landowners for petroleum production from beneath their lands, prosperity to the Mt. Pleasant area, sheilding the town from the worst financial woes of the Great Depression. Fascinated with the burgeoning industry in the face of financial depression, and it's positive impact on the area, Lyon covered the industry dilligently for the local newspaper. Probably it was he who coined the phrase "Oil Capital of Michigan" to describe Mt. Pleasant. The famous Struble well fire of 1931 (Michigan's worst oilfield disaster which killed ten people, mostly local) brought Michigan's oilfield to national attention and made Norm Lyon an oilfield reporting icon. In 1936, Lyon left the newspaper to edit the fledgling local weekly magazine the Michigan *Oil & Gas News*, returning to the *Times-News* in 1947. Lyon served 12 years, 1947-1958 on the Mt. Pleasant City Commission and was Mayor in 1951 and 1952.

In 1954, he went to work for the Mt. Pleasant Chamber of Commerce and was that organization's Executive Director until 1957, when he returned to the Michigan *Oil & Gas News* where he remained until 1972 retirement. After his retirement, Lyon served as Contributing Editor for the *Michigan Oil & Gas News* from 1973 to 1981 and wrote a weekly column for that magazine until 1985. In 1974 he was honored for his lifetime achievements by the Michigan Oil And Gas Association (MOGA) with a "Norm Lyon Night" which drew friends and associates from nationwide. Lyon is shown *left* with MOGA President Frank L. Mortl in 1980.

Extremely outspoken, Norm's gruff exterior thinly masked a devoted family man, community booster an ability to present complex serious issues in a manner that made you smile thinking about his observations. I first met Norm when I was a high school part-timer in the pressroom of the old *Daily Times-News* in 1957 and it was my priviledge to serve as his replacement as Editor (and associate/employer) at the *Michigan Oil & Gas News* from 1973 until 1985. Further, it was my honor to be his friend, fishing companion, and chronicler of his career as a true local hero.

THE MORNING SUN – MAY 22, 2011

Mt. Pleasant's Riverside Cemetery Civil War Monument to celebrated two Important Anniversaries in 2011.

On Memorial Day 1886, the Wa-Bu-No Chapter of the Grand Army of the Republic (G.A.R.) dedicated a Civil War monument (granite markers in foreground) presented to them by the citizens of Mt. Pleasant, making the granite part of the memorial **125 years old in 2011**.

Twenty-five years later, on Memorial Day 1911, the 23-foot tall soldier's monument was placed by the Wabon Post, John A. Harris Commander, making the cannonball/flagpole monument **100 years old in 2011.**

(The author is grateful to Mt. Pleasant's Joyce McClain, whose diligent research solved the mystery of the monument's origin with two Isabella County Enterprise articles dated May 21, 1886, and May 26, 1911.)

St. John's Episcopal Church 125th celebration in 2009.

Five years after Isabella County was officially organized February 11, 1859, the village of Mt. Pleasant was incorporated in 1864. In 1869, the area's first Episcopalian settler, Edward A. Audin moved to the village of Mt. Pleasant and began holding services at home for his family, soon joined by other families of the same religious persuasion. In August, 1869, the first recognized Episcopal service was held in Mt. Pleasant's Methodist church by a Midland minister and later that year Edward Audin was licensed as a lay reader by the Episcopal church and services were held in homes, then a rented hall until 1882 when constuction began on the present St. Johns Episcopal Church at the northwest corner of Washington and Maple streets in Mt. Pleasant. That building (shown above in a timeworn postcard view sometime in the early 20th Century and below in 2006) was consecrated January 20, 1884. St, Johns church is the oldest continuously occupied public building in Mt. Pleasant and in 2009 pastor Reverend Wayne Nicholson and St. Johns parishoners celebrated the 125 anniversary of the church's consecration.

Rural cabin moved to West High Street to serve Girl Scouts.

The Jane Harris Isabella County Girl Scout Cabin was originally erected along the Chippewa River southwest of Mt. Pleasant in 1938 by Edward O. Harris (of the Harris Milling Company family) and later named for his daughter Jane, who died in 1953). Being isolated, the cabin was subjected to a lot of v andalism and was abandoned as unusable. From 1949 to 1955, the scouts met in the Scout Room on the second floor of McFarlane Dairy at 424 South Mission Stret in Mt. Pleasant., In 1951, Scout Commissioned Audrie Batson and Central Michigan College Comptroller Norvall C. Bovee spearheaded a $10,000 fund drive to move and up[grade the cabin at a location on City of Mt. Pleasant property along the Chippewa River in the 1700 block of West High Street (now Chipp-A-Waters Park). On September 21, 1951, above, the cabin was moved. Consumers Power and Union Telephone lifted and cut wires along the route at no cost to the scouts to expedite the move. Moving cost by Chelsea Utterback were $850 and reconstruction of the stone fireplace cost was $550. After a few years of community volunteer labor in making improvements to the Jane Harris Girl Scout Cabin, including adding a basement, it was formally dedicated June 6, 1955 and remains in service today. The cabin will accommodate 32-40 persons.

The "lost" log cabin of Central Michigan University, gone 50 years; artifacts of alumni cabin museum in limbo.

Once nestled in the woodlands of the eastern portion of the Central Michigan College campus, an 1800s hand-hewn log cabin known as the Central Alumni Museum, nestled in the forest facing Franklin Street *(location 1 in the photograph below)* on property owned by the Central Alumni Association. The cabin, purchased in 1923 from Deerfield Township farmer Charles McCarthy, was outfitted by CMU former Dean of Women Bertha Ronan in a pioneer theme and housed artifacts typical of the frontier family's abode. One of the earliest log cabins in the county, the "Alumni Association land" east of Franklin street was purchased by Central and was the site of the first Alumni Field (below).

For many years the cabin served as a meetingt place for alumni groups, college organizations and local Boy Scout and Girl Scout organizations. In 1949, plans were made for a state of the art fieldhouse to be located near the corner of Franklin Street and Preston Street *(then all residential on the south side)*.

"$150 cabin to make room for $1,000,000 fieldhouse" proclaimed a 1950 Mt. Pleasant Daily Times-News headline. Finch Fieldhouse was built and the Alumni Museum log cabin and contents were moved across the street to the college woods behind Warriner Hall *(location 2 in the photo on the right)*.

All was well ….. until 1959, when the cabin was dismantled to make room for the new University Center and the woods disappeared. Also disappeared was the dissembled cabin, as well as the artifacts contained therein, apparently. Clarke Historical Library Director emeritus John Cumming was told the artifacts were in the basement of Ronan Hall when he came here in the mid-1960s., That was the last clue to the mysterious vanished log cabin in the woods of Central, until recent inquiries found that the cabin allegedly located on a property in western Isabella County.

W. B. DEIBEL PHOTO furnished by JOE CASCARELLI

THE SACRED HEART CATHOLIC CHURCH 1935 FIRST COMMUNION GROUP consisted of *(left to right)*: *First row – Mary Ann Lasko, Charlotte Campbell, Teresa Hickey, Mary M. Brondstetter, Audrey Smith, Lillian Fortino, Kathleen Strauss, Margaretl L. Lowther, Joan Sova, Madonna L. Kirkey, and Ann Hackett.*
Second row – William McDonell, Ronald Doerr, James Lenon, Walter Heintz, John Walker, Joseph Cascarelli, William Sheppard, John Hagan, Edward Anderson, Norbert Hall, Robert Fate, Gerald Murphy, Thomas R. McNamara, William Sweeney, James Campbell, Stanley Dole, Robert Davis, and Glenn Voisin.
Third row – Mary Bechtel, Marie Anderson, Elizabeth Hackett, Mary J. Cuthbert, Charles A. Deibel, Paul Fortino, Thomas Horvath, Raymond McNamara, Thomas Powell, William Eckert, Robert Evans, Leona Windel, Catherine Keller, Virginia Torpey, Anna Marie Mahaffey.
Fourth row – Mary Louise McCarthy, Mary Wadolowski, Helen Szekeres, Rose Ellen Quillen, Joan Moeller, Erlinda Rodriquez, Joseph Rodrequez, Ladisloa Wadlowski, Margaret Fortino, Ruth L. Ball and Elizabeth McDonald.

300 block of East Michigan - Looking northwest from the corner of Illinois and Lansing streets, the Sacred Heart Catholic Church, parsonage and school is seen in 1906. The school was replaced by a brick structure in 1908,.The church and rectory configuration worked for several decades until enrollment of Sacred Heart Academy and the moving of Mt. Pleasant High School, to the southeast outer reaches of town on Elizabeth Street, caused the need to expand the Academy's physical plant with a new elementary school building, gym and parish hall taking the place of the church and parsonage . The entire complex moved exactly one block east and just a touch to the south in 1970, below, with an almost identical juxtaposition of church and administative buildingsin the 300 block of South Fancher Street.

Building the Mt. Pleasant Post office in 1919.

The United States Post Office building, below in the 1940s, at Mount Pleasant was approved for construction at the southeast corner of Normal (later College, now University) and Michigan streets in 1913. World War I and its strains on the Federal budget delayed erection of the building until 1919, above. Building of the foundation of the Post office, viewed from the southeast looking northwest at the Michigan/Normal Street intersection, provides a rare look at the fire tower atop the old Mt. Pleasant Fire Department (center) and the five year-old Johnson's Garage, later to morph to a Ford, then Studebaker dealership where the Isabella Bank branch drive-up office now stands.

The location served as a post office from 1920 until the late 1960s, when it moved to the 208 East Illinois Street. In 2003, the Post Office moved to the north end of Main at Pickard Street.. That building is now the Mt. Pleasant Public Veteran's Memorial Library Annex.

The University and Michigan building was offices for Mount Pleasant Public Schools until the late 1990s and is now an office building.

![Central State Normal School, Mt. PLEASANT, MICH.]

1903 brings first automobile to Mt. Pleasant.

Restaurant owner Bert Gruner was the first Mt. Pleasant resident to own an automobile, a 1903 Oldsmobile. The photo *above* is believed to be Bert showing off his new ride in front of the the Central State Normal School Administration Building (later known as Old Main), the fledgling Central Michigan University's single building until 1905. The center tower with the cupola was built in 1892, with wings added in 1899 and 1902. The entire wooden structure burned to the ground December 7, 1925 and was replaced by Warriner Hall in 1928.

Mt. Pleasant Motor Co., Inc.

Right, an advertisement for the short-lived Mt. Pleasant Motor Company, which lasted for only a few months in 1914. Then-Mayor Deuel owned one one of the automobiles and claimed to get twenty-two miles to the gallong with it.

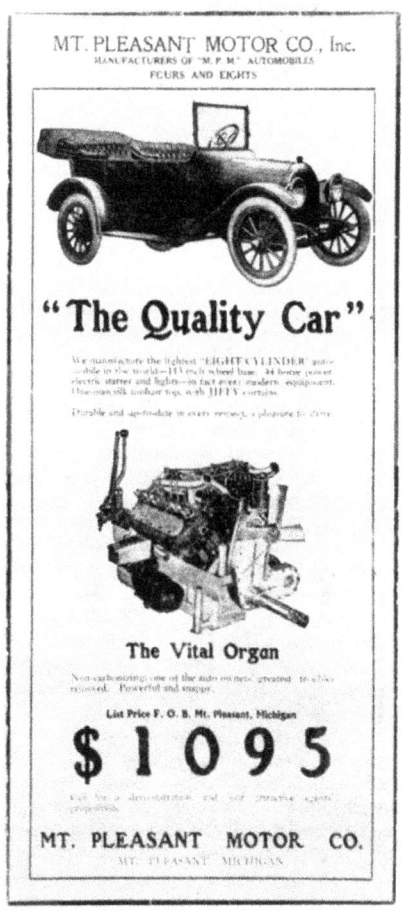

Mt. Pleasant's Transport Trucks built 1919-1923.

Building hosts manufacture of cars, parts and newspapers.

711 West Pickard – Built in 1919 as the Transport Truck Company, which operated until 1921 at this location, producing truck, taxicabs and fire trucks, the building became American Enameled Products in 1926.

Ferro Stamping Company, shown *right* in 1947, manufactured automobile parts here beginning in 1937 and tank parts during World War II before returning to car parts after the war. The plant closed in the early 1980s.

In 2010 and today, the building is now the Commerce Center, *left*, housing among others, the Mt. Pleasant daily newspaper *The Morning Sun*.

THE MORNING SUN – JULY 21, 2010

Downtown Car Shows.

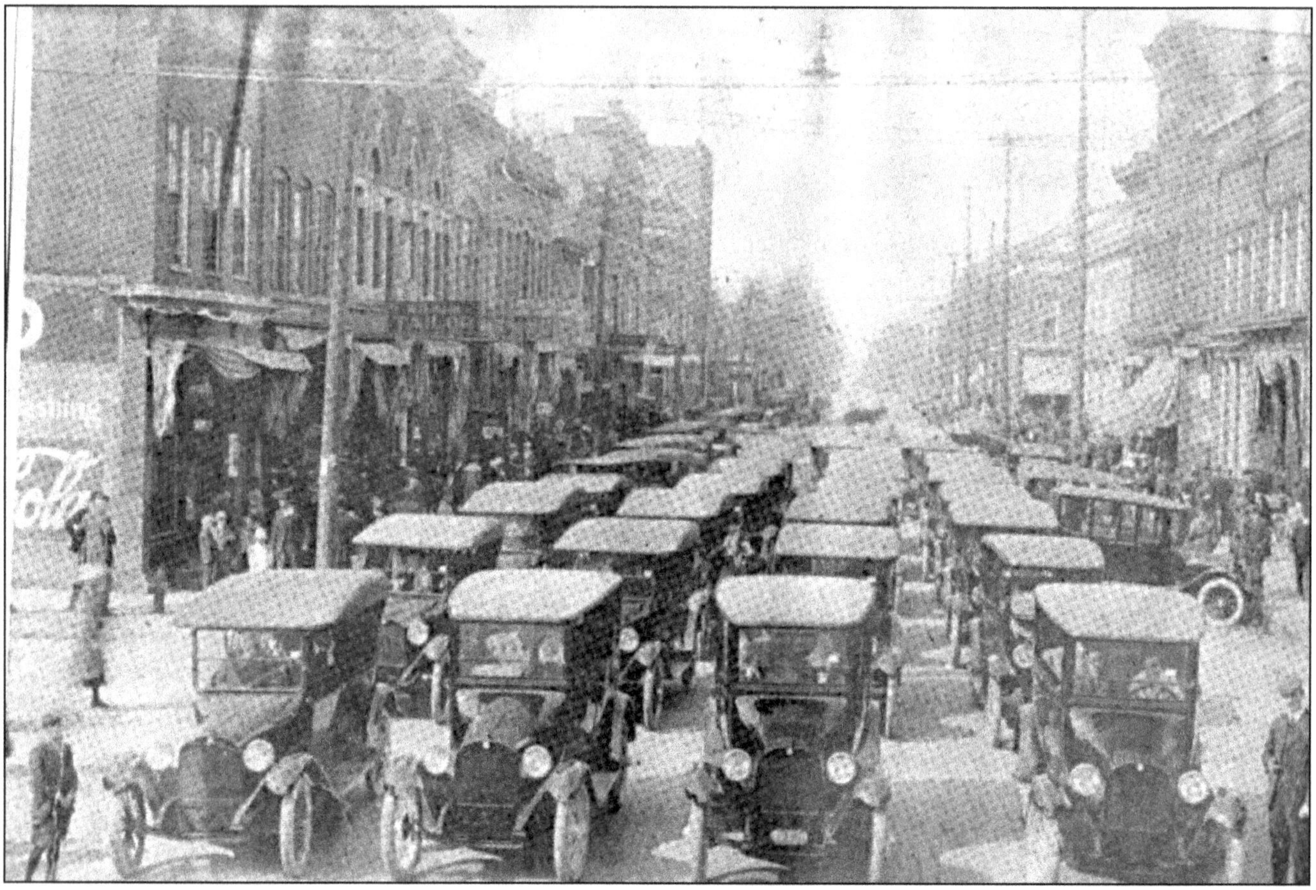

In 1918, *above*, Martin Naumes displayed his stock of 1918 Dodge automobiles four abreast and eight deep in the 100 block of East Broadway. Naumes sold cars until his 1938 death. His son Bernard had Naumes Motor Sales at 200 North Mission, which became Hartman Motors, Burgers, and is now Shaheen Motors. Fifteen years later, *below left*, Clarence Hart displayed his inventory in front of his dealership in the 200 block of West Broadway in 1934. Nineteen years after that, *below right*, over at the corner of Michigan and College (now University) streets, Floyd Johnson displayed his 1954 Studebakers in 1954.

Not pictured here is the Leo Beard Lincoln Mercury dealership at Main and Illinois nor Krapohl Ford on Court Street. Presently, no downtown car dealerships exist.

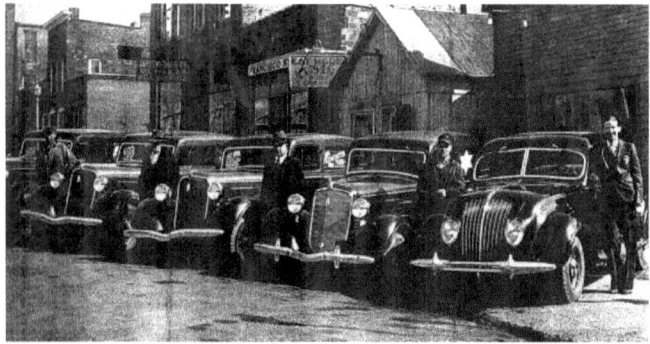

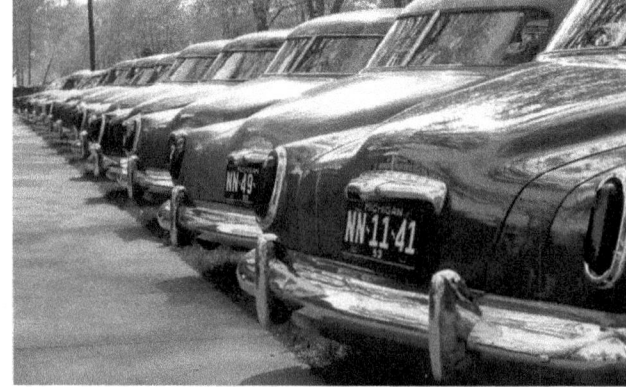

Law enforcement traffic control experiments.

In the aftermath of World War II, both Mt. Pleasant and Central Michigan College saw a decided increase in population and resulting influx of automobile usage. The increased auto use began to cause traffic control problems, dealt with in a variety of ways by city officials. In the early 1950s, *above left*, Mt. Pleasant City Manager Al Kronbach and Police Chief Vernel Davis thought they found a solution to traffic flow problems at the intersection of Broadway and Main Streets. The photo on the *right above*, finds the "No Turn" sign being ignored. Both above scenes are looking east from the Broadway/Main intersection. After several evolutions of traffic lights and blinkers, the intersection is now served by four-way stop signs …. until somebody comes up with another "better" idea. A few years later, near Mt. Pleasant schools, *right*, the city tried free-standing "School – Drive Slowly" two- sided warning signs. Again, Chief Davis posed with the latest traffic control problem solution … this time on Mission (then U.S. 27) and Andre Street near Kinney School. If memory serves in less than a year, attrition by vandalism and larceny caused the signs to disappear while mischief caused the stalwart uniformed tin traffic guards to show up in a number of places unrelated to schools.

The Mt. Pleasant Police Department 1950s "Tricycle".

Mt. Pleasant Police Chief Vernel Davis seemed to have a number of ideas for Mt. Pleasant traffic control in the 1950s. Davis, right above, implemented utilization of the three-wheeled "scooter" for more manuverable traffic control, being inspected here with Officers Fred Bell and Art Oles. Years later, the vehicle would suffer a irreparable mishap at Island Park, under officer Wayne Van Dyke.

Mt. Pleasant Police Chief Vernel Davis, supervising the auto safety inspection lines, *left,* was also vigilant about the condition of cars on the road, as attested by the random safety inspection lines set up periodically throughout the city to check the condition of brakes and lights.

A brand new 1956 Speed Trap: technology trumps lead feet.

Mt. Pleasant City Attorney Edward N. Lynch, *left abovet*, had a six-member jury observe speed-time operation in November, 1956, as prelude to a jury trial in which a motorist had been tagged by Mt. Pleasant's new "semi-robot" cop and protested the ticket.

Officer Maynard Pickens operated the machine for, *left to right beyond Lynch*: Officer Tom Martin, Officer Ray Harless, Attorney Ray D. Markel, Defendant Gordon McKinnon, Judge James E, Ryan, jurors – Kenneth Elliott, Jessie Haight, William Downey, Joy Allswede, Louise Bissett and Leona Quinlan, Attorney B. A. Wendrow and Police Chief Vernel Davis.

The exact location of the test, and the speed trap, was not disclosed.

803 South University birthplace of Isabella County Daughters of the American Revolution Chapter.

803 South University was Normal Avenue when this Colonial-style home was built by Kendall Page Brooks in 1910. The front elevation is a direct copy of the original home of Governor Bradford of colonial fame, who was a lineal ancestor of Kendall Brooks, whose family originally came from New England.

It was in this house on February 22, 1912, that Kendall's wife and her live-in mother Cynthia M. Page Brooks, Gratia and opened their home to a group of ladies interested in forming a local chapter of the Daughters of the American Revolution, which resulted the organization, of the Daughters of the American Revolution of Isabella County, pictured below in 1924.

Left to Right. Top Row: Amanda Sickles Bates, Emma Sickles Hall, Anna Coutant Crittenden, Mrs. J.J. Cowin, Nella Moss Cooper, Edith Lee Crippen, and Jennie Richmond Chamberlain. 2nd Row: Addie Woodin Coffin, Jennie Sickles Parker Thiers, Dede Sickles Rankin, Cynthia M. Page Brooks, Blanche L. Irish Gardiner, M. Louise Converse, Lorena S. Barber Larzelere, Elizabeth Irland Beddow, Margaret Anderson Ringstad. Seated on Floor: Bessie R. Fancher Tambling and Gratia Dunning Brooks.

ORIGINAL INTERVIEW APPEARS IN "THE BIG PICTURE BOOK OF MT. PLEASANT MICHIGAN" - 2010

Mt. P. West Side loses Senior Ambassador Bill Burden in 2013.

700-702 South Adams – The West Side most active senior Ambassador is Bill Burden, who turned 103-years old in August, 2010. He celebrated the week by "sidewalk superintending" the re-paving and curbing of High Street.

When Bill Burden moved to 702 South Adams Street in 1930 there was no water, sewer, or electric service in 1930, the High Street Bridge crossing the Chippewa River was still eight years away and getting to downtown Mt. Pleasant involved a circuitous route seven blocks south to Broadway Street, the nearest bridge to go east.

Born in Ohio in 1907, young Burden was a rig builder there before coming to Michigan at 23 years old when the lure of the prolific Mt. Pleasant Oilfield was providing work in the job-starved Great Depression. He moved away, got married and came back to buy the house at 700 South Adams for $700.00 in 1933. He has lived there ever since. "When we first moved here we had a clear view across the millpond and the trains coming through on the other side." Bill says. A clever tinkerer and innovator, he built a model drilling rig in 1934 for the 1935 Michigan Oil and Gas Exposition and traveled the state with the model in a special-built trailer to fairs and expositions throughout Michigan

Jack-of-all trades, Bill left the oilfields when World War II slowed the oil business to a temporary crawl as men and materials went to the war effort.

Bill Burden stands between the two South Adams Street houses he has alternately called home since 1930.

He was in the construction business for many years, working on such projects as Ganiard School, Barnes and Barnard Halls at Central Michigan College and the Frank Lloyd Wright-designed house and church in nearby Alma, Michigan. It is part of local oral legend that Bill figured out how to curve the wood for the pews in the church to conform to Wright's design.

For many years after retirement nearly four decades ago, Bill pursued his hobbies, amongst which were building motorcycles, tractors and scooters. Any nearby construction, including the building of the pavilion for Millpond Park, the Isabella Community Soup Kitchen and Freddie's Tavern across the street, as well as all the millpond landfill businesses facing High Street, found Bill front row center to watch. He's still the "go to guy" if the Soup Kitchen encounters a construction problem to be troubleshot.

Marie and Bill Burden look over the newly refurbished oil rig model Bill built in the 1930s October 9, 2009, with daughter Betty (Coomer) and son Don. Don did the model reconstruction work.

With his wife, of nearly 80 years, Marie, Burden lives in Michigan summers and in Florida winters, while keeping in touch with the world via the internet. Yeah, he's made himself computer literate.

Still ready to discuss events of yesterday or three quarters of a century ago with equal sharpness and lucidity of detail with any and all, Bill's mobility slowed only slightly by age and a recent need for a stint in the heart, doctors thought he was about eighty when they operated early in 2010 in Florida. But he used the motorized wheelchair sparingly, walking most of the time. In early 2009, when the author visited him in Florida, he had just come off the roof from trimming an overhanging tree branch that annoyed him.

Bill Burden, Mt. Pleasant's own Energizer Bunny ... died February 28, 2013.

THE MORNING SUN – DECEMBER 28, 2011

Last of the Roosevelt Refinery buildings falls to progess.

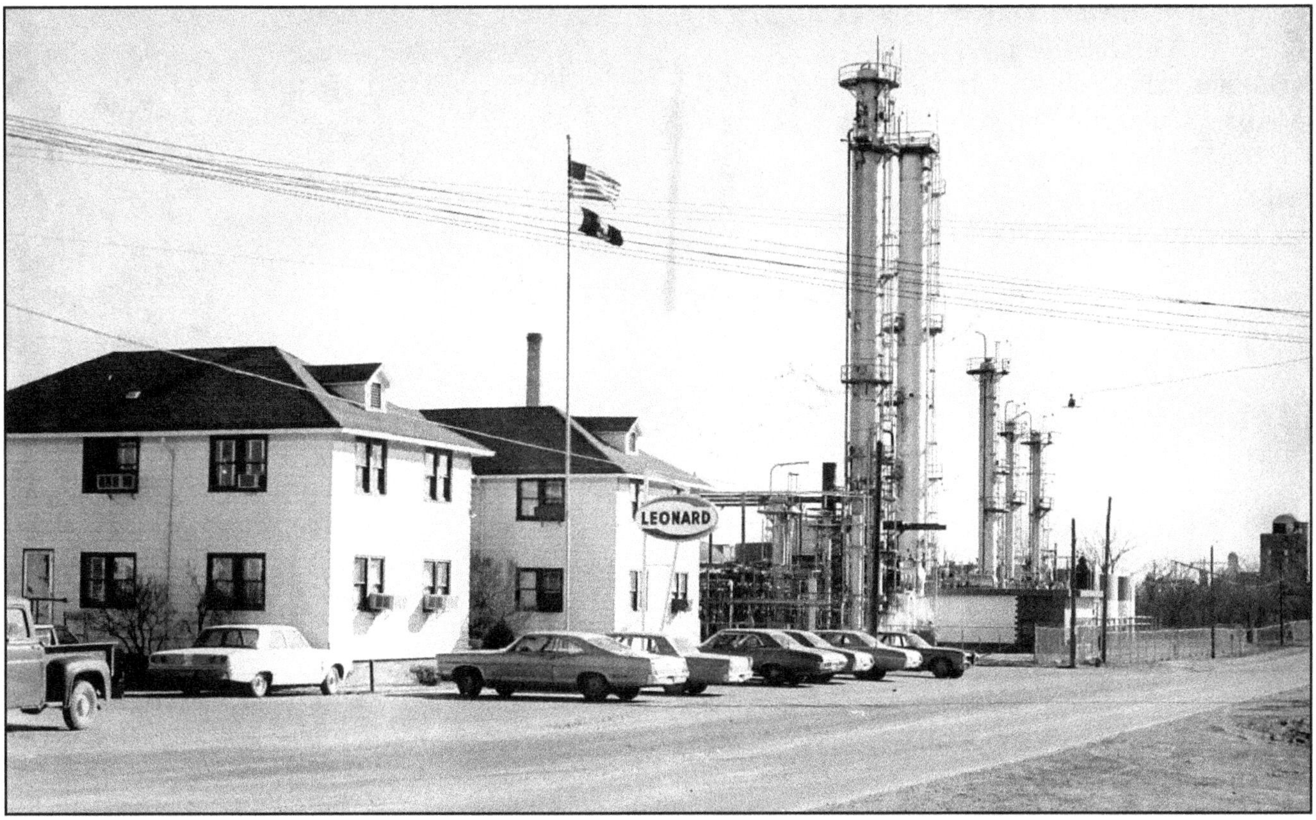

600 West Pickard – Originally occupying the area**,** 300-700 West Pickard Roosevelt Refinery, built in late 1928 and early 1929, alongside the railhead at Mt. Pleasant, was the deciding factor in bringing oil production from central Michigan oilfields to the community and establishing the community as the "Oil Capital of Michigan". Later, Roosevelt Refinery became Leonard Refineries, with it's main office building at 600 West Pickard, *above in the 1960's*.. Leonard Refinery became Total Refinery, then closed in the 1970s. In 2011, *below*, the refinery main office building was an office building housing, among others, the Michigan Oil & Gas News weekly magazine offices. In early October, 2011, the building fell to the wrecking ball to make room for a new office building, with some tenants of the old building moving to the McGuirk Building, *right in bottom photo*, while the new building was finished.

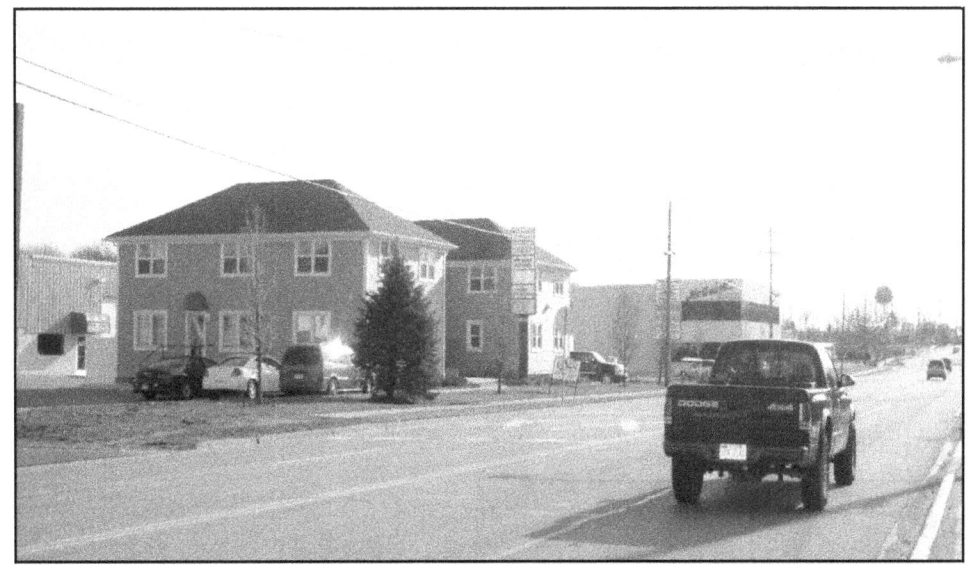

Historic Mt. Pleasant North Main Home revitalized as a B & B.

309 North Main was the home of Dr. Sheridan Ellsworth Gardiner, who graduated from the Medical College of Philadelphia in 1893 and practiced medicine in his native New York state before coming to Mt. Pleasant and establishing offices above Dittmann's Shoe Store at 133 East Broadway in 1898. In 1944, the office was moved to his home. "They made me move to the house when they thought I was going to die" he is quoted as saying in a 1956 newspaper article when he was determined by the American Medical Association to be the oldest active medical practitioner in the United States.

Gardiner organized the first Isabella County Medical Society and was its secretary for many years. Later Clare and Gratiot counties were included and the organization became the G.I.C. Medical Society, of which Gardiner was president in 1918. He was elected delegate to the Michigan Medical Society. Dr. Gardiner was Mt. Pleasant City Health Officer for about forty years. He was also secretary of the United States Pension Board. None of those laudable duties swayed him from treating patients. He made house calls throughout the county until he was 70 and house calls in the city until he was 80. After that he focused on the work of an oculist.

Gardiner's wife, *left in the photo to the right*, the former Blanche Irish, died in 1954 and her niece, Dorothy Irish, *center,* came to live with them in 1927 and remained as Gardiner's assistant. Blanche died in 1954. In 1956, S. E. Gardiner married Dorothy. He died at home, at 94 years of age, November 23, 1959, having actively practiced medicine until just a few weeks before his death.

In 1963 was sold to Verda Marie Davis, a single working mother of four and sister to Mt. Pleasant's first Chief of Police Vernell E. Davis, who served in that position from 1945 to 1959. Verna Marie Davis lived here with her mother Magdalena, The house remained under the ownership of Verda Marie Davis *(later Gwaltney)* until her 2007 death. Verda Marie married widowed contractor Charles Oakley Gwaltney in 1978, formerly of Indiana, and they lived in this house until his 1999 death. The property remained in the Charles and Verda Marie Gwaltney Trust until 2009. In 2010, the house was sold to the City of Mt. Pleasant Economic Development Department.

In 2011, the home has been completely transformed into Jean Prout's Ginkgo Tree Inn Bed and Breakfast and River Bluff Bistro, an establishment lending grace to the old neighborhood.

202-204 Court Street Brondstetter Hospital – Mt. Pleasant's early medical care needs were served by doctor's offices in the doctor's homes or small offices in downtown buildings. Doctor Michael F. Brondstetter, *far left in above photo*, purchased the house in the center at 202 Court Street from Dr. J. Franklin Adams and converted it to a hospital in 1915. Dr. Brondstetter died in February, 1931, at age 46, and the hospital was sold to Dr. L. F. Hyslop in 1932. Later, the Dr. McArthur- Dr.Strange partnership built a two story building just north of the Brondstetter hospital building, replacing the house at the left in the top picture.

Built in 1936, the new McArthur-Strange Hospital at 204 Court, *right,* was two stories high, adjacent to the Brondstetter Hospital at 202 Court. Known as the Wood Building, the new structure was used for doctor's offices, storage and labs for the original Brondstetter Hospital.

202 Court was razed to accommodate, the push-through of Mosher Street to Main in the 1970s. In 2010, *below*, the Wood building is occupied in the southwest corner by Tom and Donna Murphy

as a residence, with the rest of the building occupied by the offices of Always Me Bail Bonds; Cindy Kaliszewski CPA and Jostens.

(1915 photo courtesy Carolyn Reihl, Delwin MI).

MT. PLEASANT MONTHLY MAGAZINE – APRIL, 2008

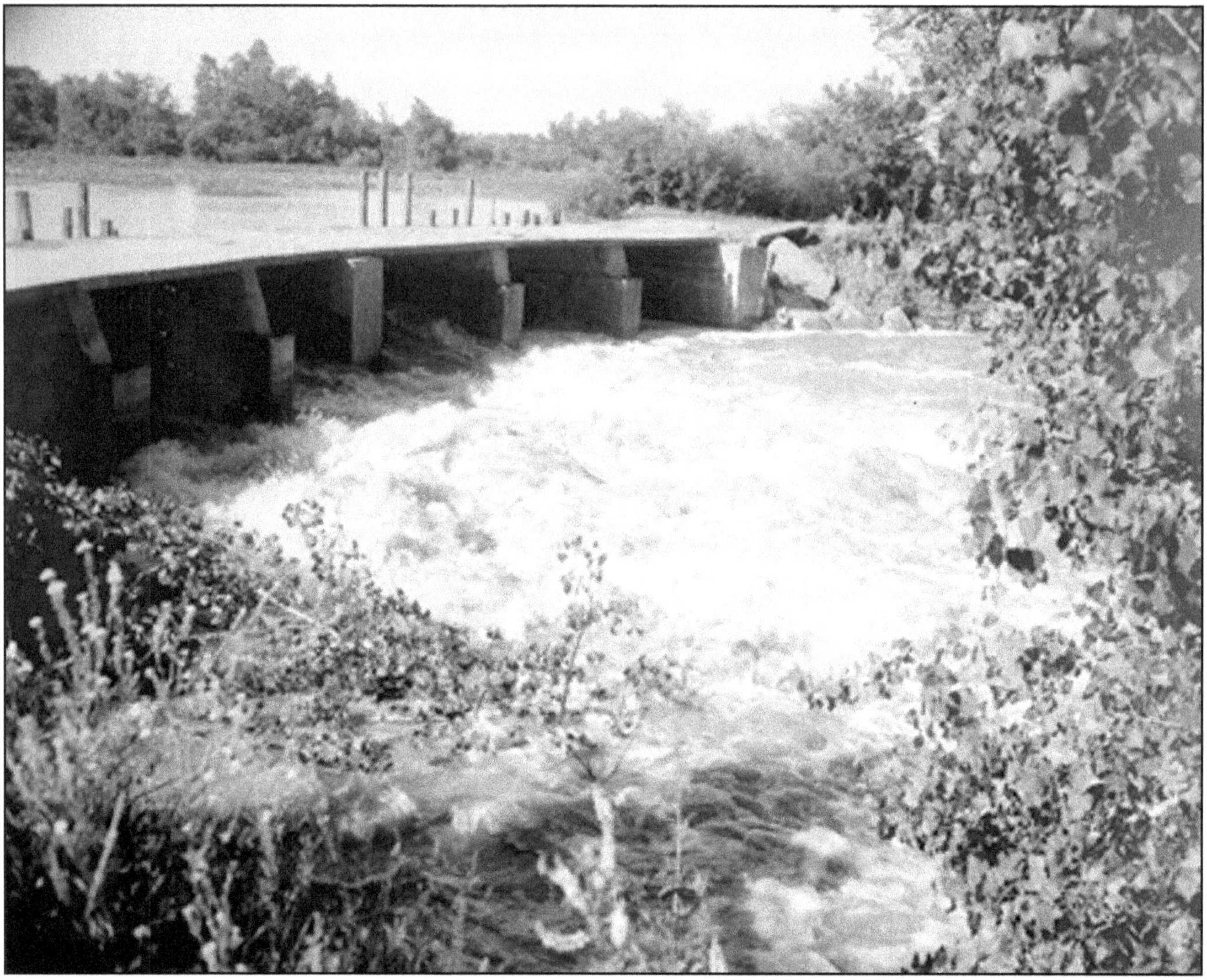

The westernmost dam *above* at what is now Mt. Pleasant's Millpond Park was once a raging torrent as melting snows and April rains poured hundreds of thousands of gallons of water from upstream of the Chippewa River into the impoundment formed by two dams and a mill run to Harris Milling Company on Broadway Street downstream. As primary outlet for the incarcerated water, the western dam provided a deep pool below the manmade "waterfall" and served as a primary spot for spring fishing. Huge tripods built from pine logs served as a fulcrum for massive nets hand-dipped into the rapids below the dam during the "sucker run" when dipnet fisherman would camp in hopes of filling the nets.

Today in spring the Millpond Park comes alive with bikers, walkers, joggers and all sorts of fisherman (without huge nets) and even kayakers and canoeists in the aftermath of the Mt. Pleasant Parks and Recreation Department's massive Chippewa River Reclamation Project .... all in wait of warmer weather when a dip in the waters from the small beach area once dominated by sucker nets once ruled the shore. Haven't been down there yet? Go!

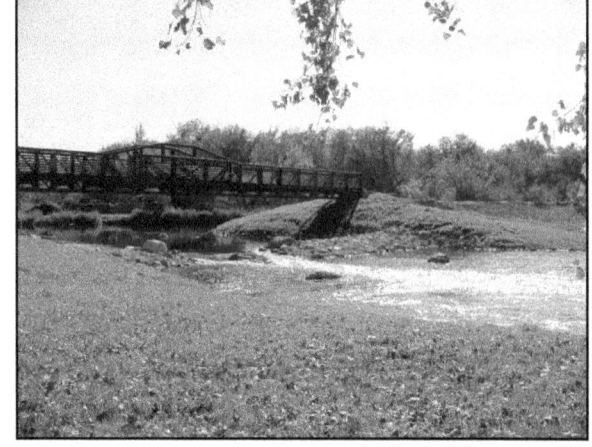

MT> PLEASANT MONTHLY MAGAZINE – MARCH, 2009

A genuine Mt. Pleasant urban legend debunked .. maybe.

Recent sidewalk and streetlight work in the 200 block of West Broadway in Mt. Pleasant brought to mind this photo from the Francisco Studio Collection at the Clarke Historical Library showing that block in the 1930s.

What appears to be smoke from a fire in this vintage picture is really smoke from the smokestack of the Bordent Building across the street.

Just out of frame to the left was something called the Bloomette Shoppe, occupying the east half of the Smithers Building (currently Mt. Pleasant Beauty School), shared with Jarecki Manufacturing Company, a maker and purveyor of tools and equipment for the flourishing local oil and gas exploration and production industry.

Second building *left*, now occupied by Fifi's, was the Francisco Photographic Studio, where Harrison A. Francisco worked in the ancestral family business until his 1973 retirement. Francisco is attributed by local oral urban legend to have disposed of a number of Mt. Pleasant pioneer photographer Eugene F. Collins' photo files in a trench in front of the studio during a sidewalk laying project when he, Francisco, acquired the files following Collins' 1954 death. Collins, came to Mt. Pleasant in 1894 as a photographer and operated his own photo studios variously on South Main Street, 117 South Washington and 501 South Mission Street until his 1948 retirement. If true, the tale of Francisco's disposal of the Collins negative files would probably not be as historically devastating as may first be imagined since the Collins studio had been razed by a 1941 fire that destroyed the most valuable negative records of the area's history.

The peaked little building third in the *photo at the right* operated as a diner type restaurant with a dozen different names before being torn down to make room for the 1960's expansion of Ray F. Cline Marketing, now Heartstrings and Fun Things at 209 West Broadway.

Help Unmask a Seventy Year-old Mid-Michigan Mystery.

The masked group above is the 1942 membership of the Mt. Pleasant, Michigan, Post of the Women's Relief Corps, an auxiliary of the Grand Army of the Republic which was formed in the mid 1880s to

"assist in every practicable way in the preservation of and making available for research of documents and records pertaining to the Grand Army of the Republic and it's members". Those records, the organization itself, and the identity of the members pictured have faded to obscurity.The organization was carried in city directories for Mt. Pleasant until the early 1950s and the closest directory we can find to the time of this photo is the 1940 editions which lists as officers: President – Minnie Montgomery; Senior Vice President – Jennie Goolthrite; Junior Vice President – Nancy Buckley; Chaplain – Mabel Dexter; Conductor – Mae Bailey; Assistant Conductor – Pheobe Kennedy; Secretary- Faith Brownson; Treasurer – Garnet Spalsbury; Patriotic Instructor - Martha Johnson; Guard – Mollie Calhoun and Assistant Guard – Margaret Bundy.

Right, the ladies pictured *above* are in the same positions without their masks. Any information about identities *(call 989-773-5741)* will be greatly appreciated and appear in a future edition of this feature. *Photos courtesy of Mt. Pleasant's Sharon Schmitt, from her grandmother, Nancy Buckley's, collection.*

Bob Heft, designer of America's 50-star flag; in 2009 was still waving the flag he designed 50 years before.

Robert "Bob" Heft of Saginaw, by way of an Ohio childhood, is hard to miss on the road in his stars and stripes-festooned van as he scurries about making public appearances and relating how, at 17 years old, he designed the 50-star United States flag more than 50 years ago.

Heft spoke September 3, 2009 to the Friends and Neighbors Society (F.A.N.S.) at Isabella County's Lincoln Township Hall, *next page*. He was at the time one of the country's most sought-after speakers with his inspiring story of personal triumph, and message of the power of determination in making personal dreams come true. An imposing "small town boy makes good", Heft's quiet demeanor belies his huge role in our country's history, he is also hard to miss in person as he radiates enthusiasm and patriotism.

In 1958, as a high school junior, Heft turned a high school history class project into a historic event when he designed the 50 star U.S. flag, which would ultimately triumph over more than 100,000 other designs to become the nation's national banner July 4, 1960. Heft's 50-star flag became the longest-serving United States flag in 2007. His involvement in the Boy Scouts of America had kindled his interest in the study of flags.

In Lancaster, Ohio, in 1958, 17 year old Bob Heft was interested in politics. There was talk at the time of Alaska becoming a state. Heft says that eighty-two percent of Alaska's population at the time were Democrats. With a Republican President (*Eisenhower*) and Congress at the time, Heft reasoned that if Alaska were to become our 49th state, a Republican territory would also need to be admitted for political balance. The majority of Hawaii's population was then Republican, giving Heft an "Aha" moment when no one was even talking about Hawaii as our 50th state. Using his grandmother's sewing machine, with no seamstress experience, Heft cobbled together a 50-star flag on the weekend for a history class assignment.

His teacher was underwhelmed and unimpressed, giving Heft a B- on the project and rejecting the flag as having "too many stars".

Heft objected.

"Get Washington to approve it and I will change your grade" Stanly Pratt, the teacher, said.

Heft, determined to prove himself right, wrote dozens of letters to state and local representatives, finally hand-carrying his letter and photos of his flag by bicycle across town to the home of then Ohio 10th District U.S. Congressman Willima H. Moeller. More than a year and a half later, Heft's design was accepted and President Eisenhaur called him at his new job (*where he had been warned about receiving personal telephone calls*) to invite him to the flag's dedication ceremony July 4, 1960, in Washington DC. Heft drove all night to get to the ceremony and drove home immediately afterward. Arriving back in Lancaster in the early morning hours, Heft took his flag to school and placed it on the desk of his history teacher. "If it's good enough for President Eisenhower, it's good enough for me." Pratt said, changing Heft's grade to an A.

Since then, Heft was a guest of the White House 14 times, known nine U.S. Presidents, appeared on countless radio and television shows and visited all 50 states, making about 200 public appearances annually. Born in Saginaw, Michigan, in 1942, Heft was raised by his grandparents in Lancaster, Ohio, not far from his friend astronaut and former U.S. Congressman John H. Glenn, where he taught high school and college for 30 years. He was also the seven-term Mayor of Napolean, Ohio, and was past president of the Ohio Mayor's Association. Heft was a state officer in the Lions of Michigan and is a member of the Downtown Saginaw Lions Club.

"Having a dream is no good if you do nothing with it." Soft-spoken Bob Heft said. "If you don't believe in yourself, how can you expect anyone else to believe in you."

Heft's talks were a "don't miss" event as he told his story in a disarmingly modest manner, laced with down home humor.

On December 12, 2009, just over three months after his Lincoln Township, Isabella County talk, sudden death robbed Robert Heft of the thrill of attending the July 4, 2010, commemorative celebration of the 50th anniversary of the official dedication of the flag he designed.

John Cumming Isabella County Historical Preservation Award.

The late John Cumming (1915-2010), *below in 1990*, was born in Shrewbury. Massachusetts in 1915 and raised in nearby Worchester. He worked as a reporter for the Worchester Telegram and Gazette until a track scholarship at what is today Eastern Michigan University brought him to Michigan the first time. After graduation, he worked for the Detroit Public Schools teaching journalism while he earned a Masters Degree in English Literature from University of Michigan. In 1961, Cumming became the second director of the Clarke Historical Library, established in 1954 on the Mt. Pleasant Campus of Central Michigan University. He worked there for 21 years, retiring in 1982.

Considered the premier historian of Mt. Pleasant and Central Michigan University history, Cumming's many published books included *This Place Mt. Pleasant* and *The First Hundred Years: A Portrait of Central Michigan University 1892-1992.*

The Mt. Pleasant Area Historical Society Founders Day Committee established the John Cumming Isabella County Historical Preservation Award in 2009, honoring CMU's Clarke Historical Library longtime director, the late John Cumming, author of many other local historical works.

So far, the award has been presented to:

2009 - Joyce McClain, Wayne Barrett, Marvin Lett, Rose Cohoon, Ben Weber, Marilyn Fosburg, Hudson Keenan, Bonnie Ekdahl, Donna Hoff-Grambau and John Cumming;

2010 – Mary Ellen Brandell;

2011 – Jack R. Westbrook and Mary Sue Sazima.

2012 – Sherry Sponseller

2013 – Val Wolters and Loretta Koester

The Cumming Award Committee meets in January to consider that year's candidate recipients for the John Cumming Isabella County Preservation Award and welcome your suggestion. The selection committee includes representatives from the Clarke Historical Library, Central Michigan University, the Mt. Pleasant Area Historical Society, the Saginaw Chippewa Indian Tribe and the Shepherd Area Historical Society.

Presentation of the Mt. Pleasant Area Historical Society's Annual John Cumming Isabella County Historical Preservation Award takes place at the closest Isabella County Board of Commissioners meeting to the actual anniversary of the February 12, 1859 establishment of Isabella as a County.

"*The leaves are crisp like autumn bunting ... the time middle-Michigan guys turn their thoughts to hunting*" ... OK, so it's not Shakespeare, but the annual hunting quest for wildlife is a middle Michigan tradition observed from the time the area was hunted by nomadic Native Americans, through the settlement by myriad ethnicities to modern times. Above left, an 1895 hunting party from Mount Pleasant prepares to brave the forests of Isabella County, *left to right* are: Chester R. Gorham, an unidentified man (perhaps a guide), Doctor Richardson, Charles McKenney and P. C. Taylor. *Above right*, Harvey McCabe displays his deer hunting success in Rolland Township in 1927. The remaining photos, *middle left and below*, were culled from the Norman X. Lyon Collection at the Clarke Historical Library and harken to the time that successful hunters posed in front of the newspaper office in the 200 block of West Broadway in Mt. Pleasant for the paper's regular hunting season publication feature.... Each presents an automotive signature of the time and displaying views of Broadway Street in the background.

MT. PLEASANT MONTHLY MAGAZINE DECEMBER, 2009

Mt. Pleasant investment advisor jars delicacy food industry with tasty, healthy autumnberry products.

In these days of financial tribulation, it's nice to have a story of sweet success here in our backyard to tell.

By day, Paul Siers is an investment advisor at Raymond James Financial Services for Isabella Bank in Mt. Pleasant. Off hours, however, Siers is putting the once-lowly autumnberry to delicious work in ways unimagined a few years ago in a small processing shed amidst a twenty acre "forest" of autumnberry trees on his forty acre farm a few miles southwest of Mt. Pleasant.

The autumnberry, a.k.a. the autumn olive, Aki-gumi (or it's dress-up name *Elaeagnus umbellata*) is a bright red round to oblong berry about a quarter- inch in diameter that grows wild on a ubiquitous invasive shrub to tree throughout much of Michigan. Imported to the United States in the 1830s from Asia for use as a soil stabilization plant in poor soil environs, the autumnberry bush *(known as the autumn olive until the United States Department of Agriculture [USDA] renamed it autumnberry to make it sound more appealing)* thrives in loamy, sandy and slightly clay-type ground, where its nitrogen-fixing root-nodules enable it to proliferate in poor soil. Drought tolerant and invasive of grasslands and sparse forest, autumnberry plants do not like wetlands or thick forest. The autumnberry bush soon fell out of favor because its rapid proliferation and, like the kudzu vine in the south, soon became a "pest plant". There it languished as an uninvited visitor to the rural landscape, whose dark green leaves and pale flowers invite deer and whose bright red berries invite birds of all sorts to dine in droves *(spreading the tough oily autumnberry seed to bring about still more fast-growing shrubs)*.

The autumnberry might well have stayed on the list of undesirable foliage if Paul and Gloria Siers hadn't bought their forty-acre spread in 1992. Gloria is an Environmental Sciences teacher at Central Michigan University and is also author of **Once There Was and Will Never Be Again**, a book relating the story of her father's early life overseas before emigrating to America. Paul is a Master Gardener. About half of their property is woodland while the other half is a former pastureland that was beginning

to be cluttered with the pesky, thorny, autumnberry trees. They set out to find an environmentally friendly way to get rid of the plants. Instead they found a healthy, tasty source of a rapidly growing line of food and drink products, flagshipped by autumnberry jam, presently being sold in about 50 upscale gift shops and, for the fifth year, being marketed as a holiday season fund-raiser by the Mt. Pleasant Rotary Club. In 2013, Siers jam was included prominently in the Rotary Clubs "All Isabella County" gift baskets.

The journey from "how do we get rid of this stuff" to a thriving fledgling autumnberry food-base processing enterprise began in 2003 when Paul learned from a fellow Master Gardener that USDA Fruit Laboratory experimental studies were finding that the lycopene-rich autumnberry can be processed into jams, jellies and sauces, as well as dried into a leather fruit. Intrigued, Siers flew to the USDA Fruit Laboratory in Beltsville, Maryland, where he met with Brent Black and Ingrid Forham who had conducted the studies, he learned that the autumnberries are among the lycopene-richest fruits known. Lycopene can reduce the risk of heart diseases, Atteroscleroisis and Cholesterol metabolism, as well as helping to prevent cancers of the digestive tract, prostate, cervix and bladder. Siers began looking seriously at processing methods for utilizing the autumnberries abounding on his property. With the help of Dave Siler of Remus, Siers was able to design, find and build his berry processing technique and, where necessary, equipment ….. some unique his Autumnberry Hill operation.

WINE, DESSERT TOPPINGS, and jam are a few of the products made from Siers autumnberry puree.
WINE, DESSERT TOPPINGS, and jam are a few of the products made from Siers autumnberry puree

"I'm a city boy from Saginaw" Siers says, "who became a farmer when I learned about the health benefits of the autumnberry. I'm also cheap, so I'm also always open to anything that can be recycled, reused, or reprocessed to be useful for all of us."Being environmentally sensitive, the Siers use no chemicals on their land and allow the autmnberry trees to grow wild. "Some have suggested that I should plant the shrubs in a line like in a normal orchard" Siers said. "But I prefer to let nature take her course. We pick by hand, process for the most part by hand, and add nothing to the basic fruit in preparation of the puree."

Autmnberries ripen in the autumn *(How's that for a surprise?)* and picking is done from Labor Day to around October 15th. Siers has employed as many as nineteen people during the harvesting and processing season.

Autumnberries ferment on the tree rather than fall to the ground. There is what's known among rural residents as "The Orgy of the Drunken Robins" -- a period of time in late fall when the antics of intoxicated bird and other wildlife add a new dimension to humorous happenings around the countryside. Taking that lead, three people, including Siers neighbor, Bill Neyer, have given Siers samples of their experimental autumnberry wine, in nuances ranging from heavy to light. The heavier, again to which the writer can attest, is a wonderfully tasty treat crying to be used as an after dinner wine.

Twelve to fifty pounds of autumnberries are collected from each bush. Sier's autumnberry harvests have ranged up to 3,300 pounds and, after processing loss and seed extractions, yielded pounds of puree. The puree is shipped to Food For Thought, an Honor, Michigan, company that makes a specialty of producing gourmet foods from organic and wild-harvested sources. Food For Thought makes a jam spread and markets "Autumn Berry Preserves" to specialty stores throughout Michigan. The jam is sixty-six percent fruit, with the remaining third of ingredients consisting on fructose and sugar. Additionally, Siers is now working with Wee Bee Jammin', a Bear Lake firm near Manistee that processes the berries, makes jam and markets it under a new label called "Ugly Agnes", a name which evolved when botany students could not pronounce the berries' Latin name *Elaeagnus umbellate*.

Although the slightly tart flavor can remind the taster of many things, autumnberries are in a taste class of their delicious own.

Another product in development is a method of drying the pulp in large quantities into a autumnberry powder to be used as an ingredient in healthy power bars and smoothies.

PROCESSING THE BERRIES – (right, top to bottom), (1) Siers uses a length of rubber hose to dislodge autumnberries from a branch into a blueberry catch frame. NOTE: Most berries are picked from the tree and brought in buckets to the catch frame. (2) Berries are loaded into a machine that blows the leaves away so that remaining berries can be transported by conveyor belt to (3) the pulper, which crushes the berries and separates the seeds from the pulp, resulting in (4) the puree.

For the future, Siers anticipates an increased demand for autumnberry products and often lectures on his experiences in developing processing techniques and equipment. Currently, he is trying to figure out how to crush and grind the fruit's seeds to make into a compound that could be used medicinally as a heart disease and cancer preventative. He saves a number of seeds each season to add to his burgeoning autumnberry forest. Siers also plans to hire pickers to go to autumnberry trees around the area and secure nearby property-owner's permission to harvest the berries, which many still consider a nuisance.

Each day brings news of another potential health benefit of autumnberry products and a growing need to redefine the autumnberry's designation as invasive nuisance. Since it is so classified, autumnberries cannot be raised as a crop for fear of aggressive infestation by seeds being spread by birds. " We actually reduce aggressive infestation because we use the seeds."

We have hopes of seeing a seedless variety being developed. One scientist in North Carolina thinks she can do it." Siers says.

As word of the health benefits fits of the autumnberry and Siers' products spread a shortage of berries could become acute. Where once it was thought the berry products dealt strictly with male health issues, indications of benefit to female health issues are coming to light.

"I'm working with a firm on the east coast that thinks they could use 50,000 pounds of autumnberries annually to process my products for the health food market. We can't plant 'em so it's been suggested that I broker them It's the old chicken or the egg issue. First I had lots of berries but no market. Now I've got market but not enough berries.."

MID-MICHIGAN HISTORY   Jack R. Westbrook

THE MORNING SUN – June 23, 2013

State Street/Jockey Alley dates to Horse & Buggy days.

State Street, between Main and Court streets just south of the Isabella County courthouse, has been persistently known as "Jockey Alley". Those conducting county business "jockeyed" for a place to park horses and carriages, *left*.

Later, automobiles replaced the carriages and the municipal parking lot continues to modern times to be known colloquially as Jockey Alley. In 1947, great hue and cry erupted from an anguished parking public when the Mt. Pleasant City Commission decided to install parking meters along the sacrosanct open parking area on the north side of "Jockey Alley", *right*. In 1948, the discovery was made that the meters were six to eighteen inches onto county land (the five acres set aside for the county complex in 1860) and the meters were removed, to be forevermore replaced by signs restricting parking time ... peace returned to the land\, *bottom right*.

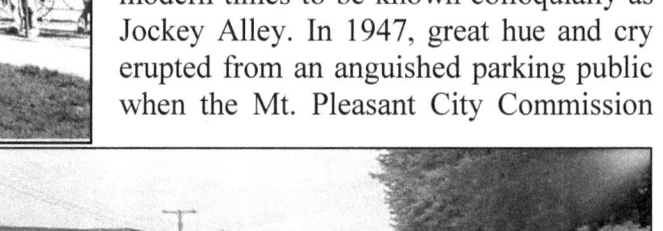

Once memories faded sufficiently, parking meters returned for a time to State Street in the mid-1950s, as shown in this view of the courthouse looking northeast, probably taken by Kathleen Peters from a window in the Campbell Building, tallest downtown structure at the time. The parking meters would finally be removed permanently when Mission Street commerce began to increase competition to downtown businesses. A "free parking downtown" slogan was trotted out as a potential customer inducement and another piece of governmental myopic

flaw in previous master plans after being subjected to the 20-20 vision of hindsight.

Mosher Street originally stopped at Lansing Street but was pushed through westward from Franklin Street, curving to join Washington at Broadway in 1974, perhaps in honor of General Mosher, who owned the property where Broadway ended at Washington Street in the original plat of Mt. Pleasant. General Mosher sold his lots to the village of Mt. Pleasant in 1878 and Broadway Street, originally called simply "the road to Saginaw" was extended west to the Chippewa River.

Bottom photo courtesy of the Coleman Peters family.
THE MORNING SUN – OCTOBER 7, 2011

Pere Marquette Fishing Club, one of Michigan's oldest, assembles in front of the club house in 1935.

The Pere Marquette Hunting and Fishing Club, with its Mt. Pleasant core of founders and members, is said to be one of the oldest … if not the oldest …continually operating fishing clubs in Michigan. Begun in 1882 and still operating, the "PM Club" is limited to 20 members who must reside in Isabella County. In its earliest days, PM Club members traveled by train as far as they could go from Mt. Pleasant to the closest station to the club's Lake County lodge along the Middle Branch of the Pere Marquette River, then hired wagons would take them and their gear to the lodge for a week of trout fishing, after which they were picked up by the wagons and returned to the Reed City train depot.

By 1935, when the photo *above* was taken, travel to the club had become simpler. The photo ran in a local weekly publication in July, 1992, courtesy of Roy Hafer. While not identified by position, the photo of the 1935 Pere Marquette Club members and guests included: W. Sommerville, F. Warner, C. Riches, E. Bixby, E. Collins, J. Ryan, W. McCall, B. Shangle, Dr. Richardson, Jack Cripo, W. F. Lewis, Walter W. Russell, W. Schnitzer Jr., D. Johnson, S. Kelly, Dr. Northway, E. Weidman and Bill Cline. The article did not contain the names of the dogs.

Mt. Pleasant pioneer John Kinney's home returns to single residency after decades of multiple family, other occupancy.

604 North Kinney *left in 1989,* was built in 1885 by Mt. Pleasant pioneer lumberman, merchant, land developer and civic leader John A. Kinney. Kinney was from Clyde Township, St. Clair County, Michigan.

In 1854, his father, Arnold Kinney, bought 320 acres near what was to become Mt. Pleasant. John worked for his father's lumber interests from age 12, and may have been David Ward's companion who stayed overnight with Mt. Pleasant's first settler John Hursh here in 1855.

Since there was no store in Mt. Pleasant goods had to be bought in from Isabella City, nearly two miles north and across the Chippewa River. In 1863, Kinney bought the log cabin at the corner of Main and Broadway and brought in goods by oxcart and canoe to open the first mercantile enterprise in town. The "Blunt" post office, four miles south, was transferred to Mt. Pleasant. With Kinney appointed the first postmaster, even though the name was not changed to Mt. Pleasant until later. In 1865, Kinney sold the store and returned to his home in Clyde Township, where he acquired a considerable amount of property and over the years served as Township Treasurer of Clyde and was nominated, but refused, State Congressional offices from that area twice.

In 1877, he returned to Mt. Pleasant and added the Kinney Addition to Mt. Pleasant and the Kinney 2nd Addition in 1884. In 1882, the first Kinney School was built in the 700 block of North Kinney, named in honor of John's civic activities and his addition to the city. The June 19, 1885, *Enterprise* announced Kinney's recent residence plans for Mt. Pleasant with the item: "Mr. John Kinney is building a new dwelling at the corner of Kinney and Andre avenues. It will be 50 x 35 on the ground, two stories high and will contain when finished 18 rooms." In 1914, Kinney subdivided the original Kinney Addition to plat the Kinney and Richmond Addition.

Kinney and his wife Margaret lived in the house at 604 North Kinney Street until 1918. In 1886, when an "Orphan Train" brought thirty-four orphaned children to Mt. Pleasant, the Kinneys were among the local families to adopt one, since four of their five natural children: Arnold, Nettie, Laura, Bertha and Marion had either grown and left home or were deceased. The adopted son, Lester, drowned.

In 1918, failing health apparently forced John and Margaret to sell the house to James and Laura Porterfield and move in with their daughter and son-in-law Bertha and W. E. Lewis at 326 North Fancher. In November, 1919, at age 82, John Kinney died at the Lewis home.

In 1920, the house sold to Hugh A. and Mary McClaren and in 1921 to Edward and Annie Axtell. For a number of years the spacious home was divided into apartments. In 1972, for instance, residents included: Farm Bureau Insurance Agent Thomas D. Carter and his wife Martha, Lease Management clerk Chris L. Henne, CMU secretary Shirley Monton, and, CMU Speech and Drama instructor William E. Valle.

For another period, the house was home to a women's shelter.

The present owners are restoring the home to its original single-home style.

1906 Mt. Pleasant Postal Service Personnel.

Top Row - Capt. C. C. Coddington, George W. Wilson; Charles D. Brown, A. W. Hance (substitute), Patrick W. Sweeney, Jas. L.Thorn, Daniel Shanahan, Peter H. Fisher, Rural Carriers.

Center Row - J. Farry McNutt (substitute city carrier), A. Frank Case (City Carrier No. 1), Charles E. Vowles (Mailing Clerk), Arza D. Coffin (Utility Clerk), Harry Hudson (Clerk).

Front Row – Frank E. Russell (City Carrier No. 2), John Garner (City Carrie No. 3), Charle A. Carnahan (Assistant Postmaster), J. W. Hance (Postmaster), Ray H. Collins (Utility Clerk).

High Street Apartment House built during Oil Boom survives.

The 1930s saw a housing crunch in Mt. Pleasant as the booming oil business here shielded the town from the worst of the Great Depression. Houses were moved here from Alma and garages converted to apartments as job seekers swarmed here from throughout the nation to work in the oil fields. Tome messt the housing demand, Patrick Haden stepped to the plate with his apartment house on High Street between Main and College streets.

The High Street Apartments at 105 East High Street, owned by Patrick Hayden, opened in 1933, *above,* with first-year residents listed as Emmett Caltrider, Harry Wilson, Jess Crontz and Blanche Scott. First housing newcomers during the Mt. Pleasant Field oil boom, the building has undergone a number of changes in appearance, *left*, and the nature of it's tenancy, with later city directory listings seeming to indicate some CMU student occupancy.

North Main Street Apartment Buildings not so lucky.

306-328 North Main The three apartment houses, two wood frame and one brick, were built to meet the 1930s Mt. Pleasant housing crunch prompted by the oil "boom" following the 1928 discovery of the Mt. Pleasant Field.

In 1947, renters of the apartments included: **306** - oilfield worker Clarence E. Glass, his wife Edna F. and Monte L., a radio technician; **308** – vacant; **310** – Mrs. Anna Estabrook; **312** – Isabella County Deputy Sheriff Ralph Langworthy and his wife Grace; **314** - William J. Coughlin; **316** – Mrs. Edna B. Maxwell; **318** – oil well driller Albert C. Hawkins and his wife Emma R.; **320** – Harold Woodin, his wife Blanche and daughter Norma Jean; **322** – Harold Chamblin; **324** – trucker Carey Robinson, his wife Lucille, daughter Colleen and son Carey; **326** – toolmaker Walter Scott Westbrook and his wife Vada *(the author's grandparents)*; and **328** – mechanic Carl G. Merrifield, his wife Clara and daughter Bonnie L.

All three structures were demolished to make room for the expansion of the Isabella County Building complex.

Home, to church, to art gallery, to church again.

319 South University - Around 1890 a group of Mt. Pleasant citizens became interested in the Christian Science Church movement. They organized loosely and formally chartered on January 15, 1891, as the Mt. Pleasant Christian Science Church, meeting in various private homes. They found that they needed a church building and they finally selected and purchased the home and site of the Richard Balmer home on lot 8 of Block 33 (319 South Church Street) on the 18th day of July, 1907.

The residence was remodeled into a very convenient and spacious church, very prettily finished, and decorated with beautiful windows. On April 19, 1908, the church was dedicated.

In 1981, several art groups in Mt. Pleasant merged to create Art Reach of Mid Michigan and acquired the Christian Science Church building, which was transformed into an art center.

In 2000, Art Reach purchased a building at 111 East Broadway, which became the organization's office and gift shop.

In 2010, the building next door at 113 East Broadway became available and was purchased by Art Reach of Mid Michigan and converted to a gallery and meeting room, with office in the back. Art Reach moved all operations to Art Reach on Broadway in July, 2010, with a grand opening held in mid-August, 2010.

The 319 South University location became the home of the Unitarian Universalist Fellowship of Central Michigan Church in July, 2010.

Rowley's buy venerable South University Funeral Home

In 1909, G. Jay Stinson moved to Mt. Pleasant and opened a funeral home on Broadway Street. He later moved into a building in the 100 block of South Normal Street. Stinson operated the funeral home there for several years with his sons under the name Stinson and Sons Funeral Home, before building a new funeral home in 1940 at 330 South Normal Street, which was renamed College Street, and eventually University Avenue. The building was dedicated in early 1941, and has been in continuous use as a funeral home since then. In addition to operating the funeral home, an ambulance service was also operated from this same building. Stinson Funeral Home was the last funeral home in the county to have an ambulance service, when it was discontinued in 1963.

Stinson passed away in 1952, and his son, Russell continued to operate the funeral home until his retirement in 1973, when long time employee Harry Helms and his wife Alice purchased the funeral home.

Helms started working at the funeral home in the early 1940's, working part time while attending Central Michigan College. He served his country during World War II, and came back to Mt. Pleasant and returned to work at the Stinson Funeral Home. After attending mortuary school at Wayne State University, he returned again to work at the funeral home. He passed away in 1980, and his wife, Alice continued operation of the funeral home until her retirement in 2010, when she sold the funeral home to long time employee, Sherman Rowley and his wife Shirley. Sherm has been with the funeral home since moving to Mt. Pleasant in November 1979. In 2010 the name of the establishment was changed to Rowley Funeral Home.

MID-MICHIGAN HISTORY   Jack R. Westbrook

tHE MORNING SUN – DECEMBER 23, 2010

503 East Broadway location served as funeral home for 61 years.

The 1890s home on the northeast corner of Fancher and Broadway streets ultimately became the J. J. Rush, Funeral Home in 1947. The Fancher and Broadway intersection, with an ever-changing series of stop signs and traffic patterns, was so prone to automobile mishaps during the Rush days, Joe Rush used to keep a broom and dustpan by the door to sweep up head and tail light glass after the wreckers hauled the cars away.

The Rush Funeral Home became the Lux Funeral Home, *left in 2006*, owned by the late Charles Lux, Senior, and now his son Charles Junior, who moved the business to 2300 Lincoln Road in 2008.

The Lux Funeral Home, along with the Helms, formerly Stinson - now Rowley, Funeral Home at 330 South University, were Mount Pleasant's only funeral parlors until Clark's Funeral Chapel opened at 113 South Bradley Street in 2000.

In 2010, *right*, the building at the northeast corner of Broadway and Fancher is occupied by the Naturopathic Institute of Therapies and Education, containing the School of Natural Health and Massage Work as well as Herbs, Inc.

Davis Clinic: Mt. Pleasant's first "medical center".

314 South Brown Street – The Davis Clinic, a forerunner of today's multi-doctor private clinics, was an association of doctors who found pooled resources and equipment assets more economical than maintaining individual offices. The clinic was formed in 1946 by Dr. Lionel Davis at 608 East Chippewa (offices later to be occupied by Dr. Ray Chamberlain and now Trinity Manual and Sports Physical Therapy). The clinic was built at Brown and Wisconsin Streets in 1952 by Fred Gannon. Dr. and Mrs. Davis lived in an apartment upstairs in the building briefly. For many years the clinic, shown *above* in 1987, was very popular. Gradually, the founding doctors retired or expired and the influx of younger new doctors faded to a trickle. The Davis Clinic closed in the 1990s. Today, the building is occupied by the offices of a variety of medical specialists.

In 1967, doctors manning the Davis Clinic included, left to right: Front row – Andrew Bedo, Andrew Velhuis, John Wood, Donald Nagler and Leo Wickert. Back Row – Paul Ringer, Lionel Davis, Lincoln Scott, Russell Ragan, John Minister, and Leroy Juhnke.

Mt. Pleasant High School 1956 CROP Drive.

The 1956 Mt. Pleasant High School Future Farmers of America (FFA) helped collect grain and cash to send overseas during CROP Week in October 1956.

Above, Ray Hoyle, right, in charge of crop collections in Union Township, and Mt. Pleasant High School Vocation Education Richard Hickman, left, outline collection plans with FFA volunteers. The volunteer group included: Roger Sheets, Alan Block, Rudy Block, Marvin Bellinger, Gary Dangler, Bob Downing, Larry Ervin, Denver Harless, Gary House, Sam Hart, Lisle Hunter, Larry Mead, Murray Morrison, Bob Neeland, Pat O'Brien, Dick Straka and Bill Thering.

tHE MORNING SUN FBRUARY 13, 2011
Isabella Community Soup Kitchen started as a class project.

621 South Adams – On a strip of land that was reclaimed from the Mt. Pleasant millpond on the east side of South Adams Street in the mid-1950s with the ill-fated idea of creating a full-fledged shopping center lies an enterprise not envisioned by the original would-be developers.

The Isabella Community Soup Kitchen became a class project of Gary Taylor while he was a student at Central Michigan University in 1990. Gary witnessed a fellow student from China eating a ketchup sandwich, the only food available to him at that time, since the country sponsoring his stay in the United States only furnished funds for books, materials, room and board but not much else for food.

Gary found no Soup Kitchen in the area and began creating one. The Wesley Foundation at CMU agreed to provide a kitchen and cafeteria. As word of the kitchen spread, more and more people came to the Soup Kitchen. In 1993, Gary found a larger facility when Trinity United Methodist Church at 202 Elizabeth Street offered its basement, where the Soup Kitchen operated for nearly ten years. Again the Soup Kitchen needed more space and the church also needed room for its programs.

A site was found to construct a new building. The new Soup Kitchen, above, with Director Genny Sobaski in front, opened its doors in December 2002. In 2003, former Soup Kitchen Lead Cook, Janet Stenman, an original volunteer, bequested a donation that helped pay off the Kitchen's mortgage.

Soup Kitchen patrons come from all walks of life: the homeless; retired people; lonely widowers unable to cook; CMU students living on a low budget; people with low paying jobs; and single parents with children; those unable to hold a job due to physical or mental illness; and young couples with small children newly relocated to the area and need a hand to get started.

The Soup Kitchen receives no government money, operation and maintenance of the facility is completely from donations by individual and corporate members of the community.

In 2010, on the average, 2,150 hot lunches were served monthly, numbers increasing during the summer.

The Soup Kitchen doors are open seven days a week, year around.

THE MORNING SUN NOVEMBER 28, 2011

Lewis B. Cole home showcases the owner/builder's skill.

(*excerpted from "At Home in Earlier Mt. Pleasant Michigan" by Jack R. Westbrook, published September, 2012)*
701 South University, *right in 1906.* This classic Queen Anne house is typified by steeply pitched, irregular roof shapes with a dominant front-facing gable was built in 1905 by building contractor Lewis D. Cole, *below*, of Cole Brothers contracting. The Cole brothers built many of the buildings at the Mt. Pleasant Indian Industrial Schools and the Mt. Pleasant Library.

His home was a showcase of his skill, which has stood the test of time, little changed externally to the present.

Lewis D. Cole was born in Lincoln Township, Michigan, and, except, for a year in Sault Ste. Marie, lived here all his life. He and wife Alice, also of Lincoln Township resided in Shepherd until building this home. Here they lived with sons Leo R., Lyle S., J. Lloyd and Reuel G. Reuel Cole would eventually become longtime owner of Coles Campus Central, buying the complex from Harry Gover.

Isaac A. Fancher, in his 1911 book *Isabella County: Past and Present*, said of the home "It has every modern convenience, is elegantly furnished and neatly kept and the lawn is a thing of beauty."

Lewis D. Cole died at 42 years old July 25, 1910, when he lost control of his automobile near Alma while on his way to Croswell, Michigan, where his company was erecting a new building. His body was found early morning beside the overturned auto. Alice Cole lived in this house until her 1953 death at 85 years old. At her funeral, the family distributed copies of the two page eulogy Isaac Fancher had written in his 1910 book.

In 1961, the Cole family sold the house to Jack and Martha Marken, who sold in 1964 to Maynard and Arline Wielenga. In 1975, the home was sold to another prominent Mt. Pleasant contractor Paul Heydenberg and his wife Carole who sold in 2000 to Craig and Victoria Battle. The Battles sold in 2009 to Ronald and Theresa Osbourne.

John Landon's last home was on South Pine Street.

401 South Pine Street – The timeworn photo above, John T. Landon tending his garden at the ornate residence he built on the southeast corner of Pine and Wisconsin streets. John T. came to Chippewa Township, Isabella County at age 22 from his native Canada in September, 1862. He worked a year for $15 a month and board for he and his wife. In 1863, he went into debt to buy 40 acres and in 1873, now a prominent landowner, lumberman and farmer, he built the county's first brick structure as a Chippewa Township residence.

He was living in this house when he died in 1912, one of 6 properties he owned in the city of Mt. Pleasant.

Dick Barz: Central Michigan Area Toys for Tots Founder
July 11, 1930 – December 1, 2013

The U. S. Marine Corps Reserve Toys for Tots began in 1947 in Los Angeles, California, when Major Bill Hendricks, USMCR, noticed that there was no charity specifically organized to distribute toys to deserving children during the traditional Chriistmas season. Hendricks gathered and distributed over 5,000 toys that year, beginning a program that became an annual nationwide effort, coordinated by the U. S. Marines.

Forty-one years later, in 1988, retired Marine Sgt, Richard A. "Dick" Barz, having lost his wife of 14 years and feeling withdrawn and distraught, attended a meeting for the survivors of the Chosin Reservoir battle of the Korean War, called "the Chosin Few", in Rankin, Michigan. There he heard about the Toys for Tots program for the first time and was inspired to action. With the help of his family, began collecting toys for distribution the first year from his business, Barz North American Van Lines, collecting, sorting, wrapping and distributing about 50 toys in Isabella County that year.

Toys for Tots became an annual family activity. Dick was coordinator as the program expanded to include Clare County. Eventually the Central Michigan Area Toys for Tots program. Area law enforcement, businesses and a growing pool of volunteers rallied to the cause. By 2006, Dick Barz, dressed in his Marine uniform, *left*, along with more than 100 volunteers, was able to distribute more than 8,000 toys to 2,400 area kids.

In modern times, toys can no longer be delivered and wrapped because of the volume of donations. Instead there is now a "Toy Distribution Day", when any parent can come and get toys for children otherwise without means for Christmas toys. Coordinators have Santa visit the children, play holiday music, give away popcorn, computer register recipients, sort and distribute toys.

Barz, whose feet and leg problems stem from his being frozen during the Chosin Reservoir campaign of the Korean War, yielded Toys for Tots coordination to his daughter Lucinda (Barz) Clark, retiring from active participation in 2008.

Barz has expressed the belief that his life was spared at the Chosin Reservoir so he could begin the program to make Christmas merrier for local kids.

As the 2013 Christmas season began, Dick Barz slipped quietly away from this life, proud of the role he played for lighting up Christmas for thousands of children.

So long, Sarge. Well done!

Mt. Pleasant Christmas in the 1950s.

The Christmas season in early 1950s downtown Mt. Pleasant, during a less "up-tight" time, began after Thanksgiving Day, *above left*, with a Christmas Parade (when it could be called that without ruffling the feathers of the rabble-rousers). The parade circumvented the downtown area to end at the Isabella County Courthouse south lawn, *above right*, where Santa awaited with candy canes and a Christmas wish listening ear, mobbed by an eager crowd to see the only Santa in town (crowd control courtesy of Mt. Pleasant Police Chief Vernel Davis.

Below, the December 3, 1954, *Daily Times-News* reported, right photo,"There will be a happy Christmas for scores of boys and girls from needy families thanks to the Fancher School PTA toy drive. Jack Clabuesch, *left*, not only contributed toys but helped man the collection box with assistants Wesley W. Merrill and Richard Millen." In the photo *right below*, volunteers box up more than 1,000 cans of fruits and vegetables donated by hundreds of children attending a free movie (in exchange for canned goods) at the Ward Theater. Technology, transportation and more aggressive marketing (starting sometime before Labor Day) have diluted the simplicity, (and some say) charm and gentility of such Christmas seasons here and everywhere.

The downtown Mt. Pleasant holiday season of the 1950s.

Christmastime in downtown Mt. Pleasant in the 1950s was the center of the town's holiday activity pre-malls, pre-big-box stores, and "pre-uptightness" about the reason for the season. In early November, the Christmas decorations were erected (to be up before deer season) but not lit until after Thanksgiving, traditional kick-off of the Christmas shopping season.

Counter clockwise from the *bottom left* are: 1 – the west side of North Main looking south (the

county courthouse trees on the left); 2- looking north on Main Street in front of the Park Hotel (today's Town Center), with courthouse grounds trees on the right; 3 – the City Christmas Tree was erected at the "T" of East Broadway and College (now University) Street just slightly east of today's Max & Emily's; 4- on the other side of Broadway looking east, that's the Bennett Hotel on the left with Breidenstein's Grocery (now Norm's Flower Petal just left of center), and the clock is on the front of Isabella County State Bank, right; and 5 – Yes, that's a nativity scene atop the Mt. Pleasant Municipal Building in the 100 block of South University.

Dare we say it …. MERRY CHRISTMAS ….. <u>TO ALL!</u>

Hooray! It's A Downtown Parade!

Autumn in downtown Mt. Pleasant was hallmarked for decades by parades. Decades before the now defunct Mardi Gras Parade, downtown was always the scene of Central Michigan University, Mt. Pleasant High School and Sacred Heart Academy Homecoming parades before some fainthearted organizers shifted "safer" venues.

In the days before electronic intrusion on real entertainment values, downtown was the scene of parades such as, *clockwise from top left*, a 1917 soldiers funeral procession passes the Borden Building heading west on Broadway to Riverside Cemetery:

1- 1955 MPHS Hormecoming parade heads south on Main Street with the Park Hotel, Campbell Building and others that used to dot the 100 and 200 blocks of North Main visible left in the frame;

2- Holiday Parade float makes the turn south on Main from Broadway in the late 1950s in front of Mt. Pleasant Hardware on the southwest corner of Main and Broadway, and;

3- 1955 float crosses Michigan Street on Main in front of Wakefield's Grocery and Spagnola's Grocery beside it (both now the Brass Café) at the northwest corner of Main and Michigan.

THE MORNING SUN FEBRUARY 20, 2011

Downtown captured by brave photographer in early 1900s.

109-117 West Broadway – Looking southeast from the Borden's condensery smokestack in 1910, the steeples in the background are those of Sacred Heart Catholic Church. In the foreground are the buildings along the south side of Broadway to Washington. The "just off Main Street" businesses in the 100 block of West Broadway have over the years included; 109 – Falsetta's first restaurant, Franklin Supply in 1947, Mt. Pleasant Supply in the 1960s through the mid-1970s; 111 - Del's Photo Service in 1947 and the Moose Club from the 1940s to the 1980s; 117 – Bailes Beauty School in 1947 and Mt. Pleasant Beauty School by the 1970s. The beauty school became M. J. Murphy's Beauty School and moved across Washington Street in the mid-1970s. For awhile in the 1970s and 1980s, 117 was the offices of Jay Woods, oil developer.

In 2010, *left*, the buildings of 100 West Broadway, south side, were occupied by the Faith Community Church.

THE MORNING SUN JUNE 5, 2011

209 West Broadway – In 1948, Mt. Pleasant-based oilfield supply firm Franklin Supply Company opened expanded operations at 209 West Broadway in Mt. Pleasant. A few years later, the firm grew to become a worldwide enterprise and moved headquarters to Houston, Texas and their Mt. Pleasant operation to Industrial Avenue before closing the Mt. Pleasant store in the mid-1960s. The empty building was purchased by advertising agency owner Ray F. Cline, who rented it for a while to General Telephone (while they completed their 301 South Main Street operation). Cline opened his sign shop division in the west side of the building *(right)* with advertising agency offices in the east wing *(left)*. Later the left wing in the photo, *right*, became the center of the building in 2011, when Cline acquired the property to the east and opened a gift store, expanding that phase of the business beyond the west side (converted to gifts when the sign shop closed). When Ray Cline retired, his ClineMark bank promotional supply business fell to son Steve, which continues to operate, while the store and West Broadway location was sold to Ray Cline's granddaughter Janelle Joslin and husband Jon. The Joslins consolidated the gift shop to Heart Strings and Fun Things in the west side while converting the east and middle to retail space, from which they operated Halloween Central for a few seasons before moving the Halloween business to seasonal rental space on South Mission. In 2013, the building is unoccupied.

100 block South University – On August 7, 1949, soundings were taken for soil sampling to test the soils integrity for placing the footings of the new Mt. Pleasant Municipal Building, *above*, completed in 1950 at 120 South College (now University) Avenue.

Businesses along the block at the time included Western Union, Enterprise Print Shop, Women's Exchange Thrift Shop, and Hal's Tots 'n' Teens, attorney Ray Markel, Stinson Agency and Dr. Baskerville.

In 2010, businesses include on the east side of the block included: Emma's women's fashions, Benefit Consulting, Central Insurance Agency, Flexible Health & Wellness, Scrubs & Such, Ross Accounting and attorneys Stein & Higgs and Janes, Backus & Janes.

Among those 1950s South College Street merchants was Hal O. Wood, a former Montgomery Ward's manager originally from Coldwater, Michigan, who opened Hal's Tots 'n' Teens clothing store at 111 South College Street in 1948. While wife Gladys taught at Weidman schools, Hal often employed his youngsters: Shirley, William J., and Judy in the store. Hal moved the business to 107 East Broadway in 1962, sold the business in 1965 and retired.

Note the "new" Mt. Pleasant Municipal Building reflected in window of Hal's store behind him, right.

A look inside Richmond Shangle Hardware.

121 South Main Street was the home of Richmond & Shangle Hardware store when this photo of Pete Lunde and Dale Shangle was taken in 1953. Later the store became the Vandyne Hardware and in 2010 is the home of Motorless Motion, a well accoutered bicycle shop in space variously occupied through the years by a Western Auto store, D & D Health Foods store and Mother-To-Be Maternity Shop. Upstairs, in what are apartments in 2010, dentist Dr. E. A. Northway practiced into the 1950s and the Isabella County Department of Welfare had offices.

The author is grateful to Mt. Pleasant's Phyllis Mc Crum for the 1953 photograph, which came my way by\way of her grandson, the Morning Sun's own Jeremy Dickman, who passed away March 5, 2012.

THE MORNING SUN - AUGUST 4, 2013

The New Yorker clothed generations of Mt. Pleasant women and children for three-quarters of a century.

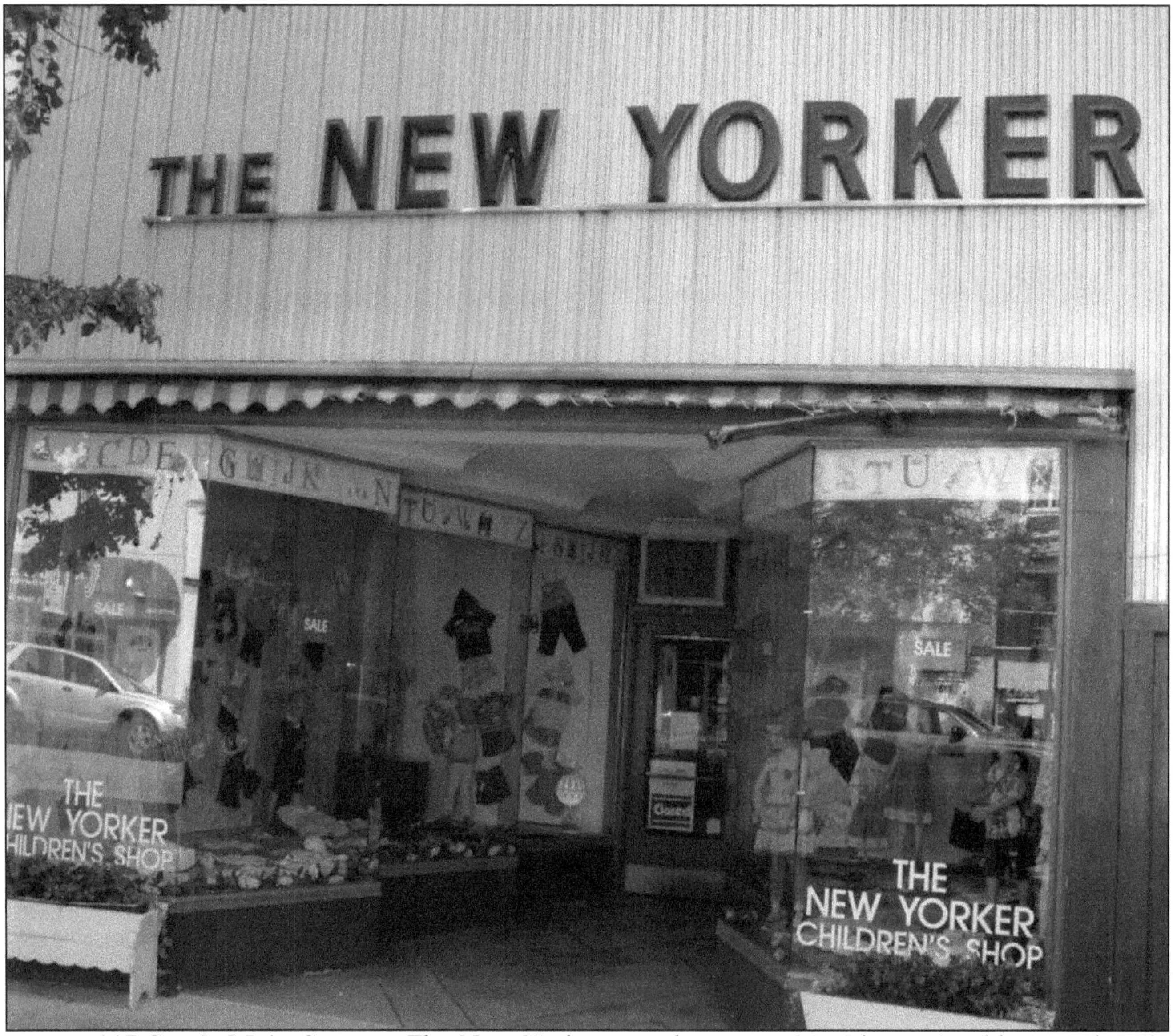

117 South Main Street – The New Yorker was downtown Mt. Pleasant's oldest continually operating retail store with the same family ownership.

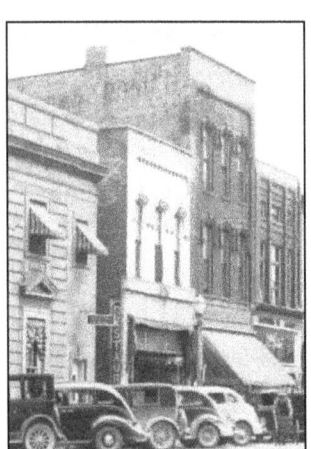

For the more than 76 years the store was open, four generations of shoppers passed through the doors.

When asked if he had any old pictures of the exterior of The New Yorker children's clothing store in 2010 owners Jack and Trudy Karr said "It hasn't really changed that much."

Les and Marjorie Karr opened the doors at this location in 1937, shown in 1930s street scene at the *left* with its signature canopy. Since its beginning The New Yorker specialized in women's and children's clothing, changing in 1975 to strictly children's wear. Other than updating styles, little changed here, including the friendly Karr welcome, a New Yorker tradition until the store closed in the spring of 2013.

Mt. Pleasant's first cement sidewalk laid on South Main Street and a "mooo-ving ride to town".

122-128 South Main, *right*, was the site of the 1904 installation of Mt. Pleasants first cement sidewalk. Note the horse-drawn, steam-powered cement mixer. For orientation purposes, starting left to right in 2010; the building signed "Provisions" is now the northern street front of the Brass Café; the "Meat & Groceries" storefront is now Mt. Pleasant Memories"; the "P. Corey Taylor – Drugs, Wallpaper, Stationery, Books" front, established in 1888, is now Ombodies; and the unsigned building, *right,* is now The Upper Cut. *Below*, apparently foot and carriage traffic approved of the South Main curb and sidewalk improvements. Note that the animal pulling the cart is a bull, which almost allowed us to "milk" the oddity in the headline.

(Top picture courtesy of Hudson Keenan by way of Loren Anderson.)

South Main Street Delivers -
John Straight keeps milk trucking alive.

202-218 South Main – In 1948, the west side of the 200 block of South Main Street, above, was occupied by: 202 - a Standard gasoline filling station, 206 – a beauty and barber shop, 208 - Thayer Dairy Bar. Baker Maxwell Walton and fireman Chief Ormond Flynn lived in apartments upstairs over Thayer's; and 218 - the Ward Theater. A Divco milk truck moves south in the lower right quadrant. Nearly 60 years later, in August of 2007, milk truck aficionado Mt. Pleasant's John Straight used his own 1964 Divco milk truck to duplicate the scene down to the vehicle in front of the theater, where a rare 2002 Japanese American Isuzu Vehi-Cross is parked. Straight says the idea of reproducing the 1948 street scene using his own Divco truck came from the author's 2006 book *Mt. Pleasant Then and Now*. John has since sold the truck but continues to lecture about Mt. Pleasant's dairy history

THE MORNING SUN AUGUST 16, 2011

200 block of East Broadway an entertainment center since 1906.

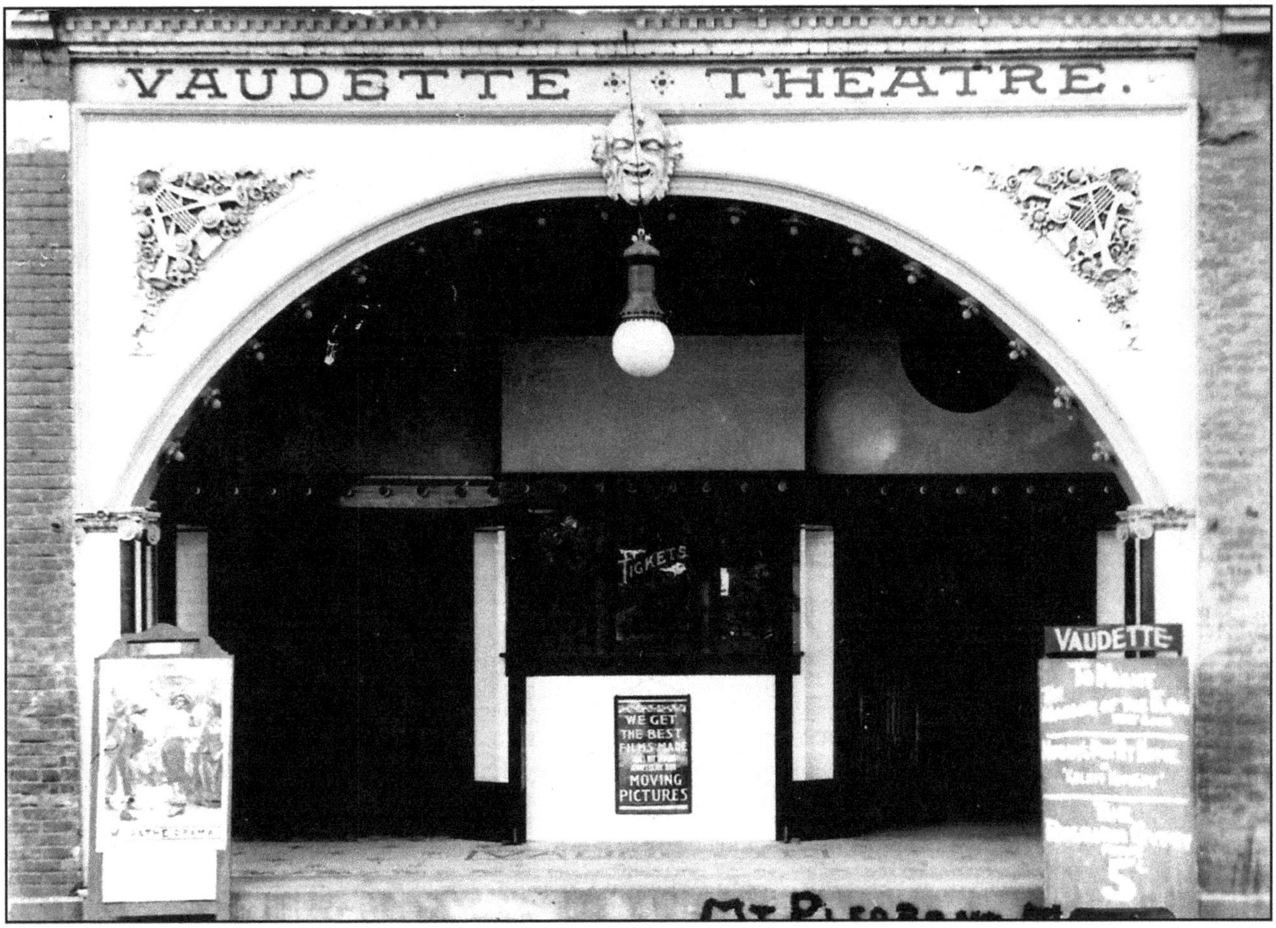

The Vaudette Theater at 218 East Broadway, *above*, was built about 1906 by Charles "Tip" Carnahan to show silent movies and stage acts. When Carnahan sold the theater to Bert Ward in 1915 to start the General Agency (insurance), the name was changed to the Broadway Theater. Bert's son Lee owned and managed both the Broadway and later the Ward until both sold to the Loeks theater chain in the 1980s, who later closed both theaters and opened the Cinema Theaters on South Mission and still later built the Celebration Cinemas on East Pickard.

In 2012, the Broadway is home to The Friends of the Broadway, a community players group that performs regularly and hosts other events. The Ward Theater is now owned by the Grace Church.

On February 11, 2012, *below*, the Broadway Theater hosted the premier big-screen showing of "Isabella County: 150 Years in the Making" as part of the Mt. Pleasant Area Historical Society's Isabella County 153rd Birthday Founders Day Celebration.

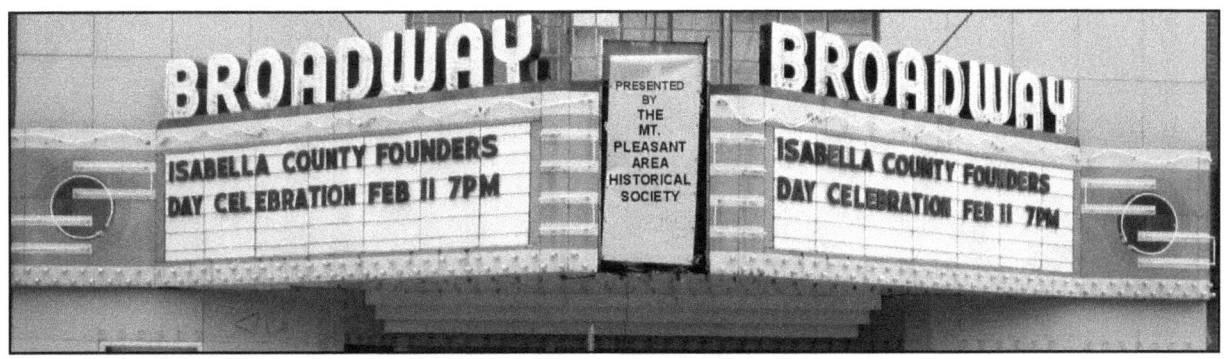

East Broadway a longtime street performer venue.

121-123 East Broadway – The occasion of the left photo is vague but it is probably a holiday street sing, which was common in earlier years. . Note girl in the far right dressed as an elf. In the background is the north side of the street, *left to right*; 121 East Broadway - Evenknit Hosiery, later Fashion City women's clothing, now Downtown Drugs; 123 – Mr. Charlie's women's apparel, the Trillium in 2010; and 125 – Tuma's Farm Market, later Scully's Jewelry, now Max & Emily's Bakery Café. In earlier days, 123 East Broadway was the site of Thad Hayling and Dan Johnson's meat market, later Johnson and Honeywell Meat Market. *Below*, actor-songster-guitarist Jeff Daniels performs August 21, 2010, in the street in front of Max & Emily's and Trillium to a crowd of more than 2,300 as part of the eatery's annual street concert series started in 2009 by Max & Emily's, Isabella Bank and Downtown Mt. Pleasant. Daniels performed here again Saturday, August 20, 2011 ad January 28, 2014.

Keeping downtown Mt. Pleasant time with Isabella Bank.

Almost from the very beginning following the 1903 opening of Isabella County State Bank, *above left*, at the southeast corner of the "T" formed by the intersection East Broadway and *(Church, Normal, College)* University avenues in downtown Mt. Pleasant, citizens of the community could set their timepieces by the clock on the Broadway facing of the banks main offices.

The gracious old "hand clock", *above center*, was the longest serving of the Isabella Bank public timepieces, teaching young downtown shoppers to tell time as they passed in their horsed and (later) horseless carriages.

The late 1970s saw a change to a bigger new-fangled digital clock face, *above right*, and the nomenclature of timetelling changed from "a quarter to" or "a quarter after" to "--:45" and "--:15." *(We've been informed by the youngers that telling time on a clock or watch with hands is soooo "old school.")*

Into the 1990s, as more bank operations moved across the street to the northeast corner of East Broadway and Court Streets, some aspects of the now Isabella Bank & Trust remained in the original building, *below left*. When the bank name changed to Isabella Bank & Trust The Victorian-era appearance changed with new cladding added to modernize the venerable old building and a bigger, bolder clock was added, still only visible from east and west approaches on Broadway.

In April, 2009, Isabella Bank completed its north side of East Broadway expansion into the building formerly occupied by D & C 5 & 10 cent store and Dittman Shoes while administrative and other offices moved to the former Mt. Pleasant City Hall building at 400 North Main Street. A feature of the new expansion is the installation of, guess what, a three-faced clock with hands, *below right*. The new clock is now visible for the first time for those approaching the "T" from the south on University Avenue, as well as east and west approaches on Broadway.

MID-MICHIGAN HISTORY   Jack R. Westbrook

THE MORNING SUN AUGUST 29, 2011
205 East Broadway … a place for "hangin' out" 7 decades ago.

Seven decades ago, 205 East Broadway was the site of The Teepee, a short-lived teenage and Central student entertainment venue featuring dancing, musical entertainment and non-alcoholic refreshments. Peggie Fuller, later to be Peggie Edmonds, is in the doorway with her friend Mavis Hagerman Peggie in the left photo and peeking from inside the teepee. They preserved their memories of their favorite place for themselves, and fortunately us, in 1943.

Thanks to Peggie Edmonds for sharing this rare shot of one of Mt. Pleasants favorite teenage icons of the 1940s.

The site was later home to Belle's Hat Shoppe, El Cove and now is the Broadway entrance to the Blue Gator, still a gathering place for slightly older youth.

Happy 1956 Mt. Pleasant!

The year 1956 dawned in Mt. Pleasant with the disreputable appearance of the junker truck, above, chained to a parking meter in front of the Mt. Pleasant City Offices at 120 South College Street *(today's University Avenue)*, which also housed the Mt. Pleasant Police Department. The door-flapping New Years greeting to Mt. Pleasant Police Chief Vernel Davis was stealthed into position by dark of night under the noses of the local constabulary.

Local oral legend, via retired Mt. Pleasant barber Richard Switzer, has it that V & M Motor Sales owner Merton Ford, who did towing for the city, was protesting what he perceived as the slow speed of city compensation to his business for the towing of abandoned vehicles.

Also according to local legend, the bill was paid promptly and the tale of this collection solicitation was added to the considerable compendium of "Mert" Ford stories.

MID-MICHIGAN HISTORY   Jack R. Westbrook

THE MORNING SUN NOVEMBER 25, 2010
100 Block of South Mission changed greatly.

1980s Photo courtesy of Agnes McDonald

100 South Mission at the corner of Mission and Broadway Streets, *above in the 1980s*, with Alswede's Restaurant at the left facing Mission Street and the used car lot of Archey Motor Sales (originally J. F. Battle, then Smale's Chevrolet Sales and now Murray Wholesale facing Broadway, where Alswedes Grocery once stood. When Mission Street through Mt. Pleasant was US Highway 27, before the superhighway opened east of town, Alswedes was a popular dining spot for tourists. In 1947, those tourists dining at the restaurant included swimming movie star Esther Williams and her husband Fernando Lamas, who stopped for lunch when Williams was on her way to Mackinac Island to film the musical "This Time For Keeps", for which the Grand Hotel built the swimming pool still in use.

Alswedes was owned and operated by Agnes McDonald in later years before it's 1977 closing, when she bought and operated Agnes's Wonderland Restaurant (the former Scotty) at 700 North Mission Street. In 2010, the 100 South Mission Street address is shared by: Suite A-Dairy Queen, B- Nail Parlor, C&D- Smokers Club, E- Gold Buyers, F- Moeggenborg Farm Bureau Insurance Agency, G- Jim and Donna's Flower Shop and H- Cash Advance, *right*.

MID-MICHIGAN HISTORY   Jack R. Westbrook

THE MORNING SUN MARCH 27, 2011
Local motorist gets a bang out of carnival arrival.

The carnival came to town with a bang in this mid-1950s news photo of a traffic mishap that drew a crowd to the corner of Mission and Broadway streets, where United States Highway 27 was so scantly traveled that folks could cluster in the northbound lane. Until August, 2006, the Sweet Onion restaurant occupied the corner immediate left for 34 years, in a building originally built by Chris Moutsatson as Chris's Drive in restaurant.. Muffler Man, Incorporated is on the southeast corner where the house with the copula stood and Rite-Aid pharmacy is located just out of the frame to the right, where the Standard sign is in this shot. Happyland was the company that furnished the rides and carnival amusements for the Fourth of July and Isabella County Youth and Farm Fair events at Island Park, where this truck was no doubt headed when he became part of this traffic jam. No word on the identity of the 1950s shorts fashion pate.

Polly's Market a Mission Near Broadway Landmark for decades.

Pauline Howard's brother Henry Neff, Pauline and Ellis Howard pose with children Bob Howard and Rosemary Neff in front of Polly's Market in the 1950s.

116 North Mission Street – Polly's Market began at the northeast corner of Mission Street and Broadway when Ellis Michael Ellis and his wife Pauline "Polly" Howard began selling fruits and vegetables to travelers along Mission, then US Highway 27 in the early 1940s. Diligence and long hours earned the market popularity among travelers and locals as a great place for fresh sausage, eggs and refreshments. Married in 1935 in Miami, Florida, the Howards started Polly's market in 1939 in Pauline's hometown, Mt. Pleasant, and it grew beyond their dreams, the business often operating 24 hours a day. Ellis Howard was killed in an oil well explosion in 1962, visiting a wellsite in which he had an interest. Traffic and shopping habits with the arrival of expressways and mega-super markets, gradually eroded the business base that had made Polly's successful. The site became the home of Chris's Drive-in and is the site of the abandoned Sweet Onion Restaurant building (razed in Nomember, 2013), as well as sharing addresses Graff Motor Sales, originally built by Ben Traines in 1956 as a lease property to Naumes Motors Pontiac and Cadillac dealership, eventually becoming Hartman Motors, then Dean Burgers Pontiac, Buick, Cadillac and GMC truck dealership, then Shaheen's Motors, and now Graff with the same makes.

The author is grateful to Sandra (Howard) Wood for photo and narrative.

Sweet Onion/Chris's Drive In building comes down in 2013.

In the late 1950s, at the beginning of the Mission Street expansion explosion, Chris Moutsatson, owner of the Olympia Restaurant in downtown Mt. Pleasant, closed that establishment to open Chris's Drive-In On the northeast corner of Broadway and Mission streets. In 1972, the LaBelle Group of Mt. Pleasant opened the Sweet Onion Restaurant at that location, founding a chain of three restaurants that all closed in the mid-2000s. This Mt. Pleasant location was demolished in November, 2013.

MT. PLEASANT MONTHLY MAGAZINE MAY, 2008

The original Pixie drive-in restaurant opened at the intersection of Chippewa and Mission streets in 1948 in the corner of the Turner-Labelle used car lot. Today's Labelle Management, owner/operator of restaurants and hotels throughout Michigan, sprang from that humble beginning. Note Giant Supermarket, another Mt. Pleasant original, in it's second location of the original store, across Mission street to the left of the photo on the right.

The September, 2006, crew of the Pixie, the cornerstone of the Labelle companies still operating at the same but expanded stand, included, *left to right*: *front row* – Dave Scholten (LaBelle Regional Manager), Erica Allen, Dawn Haggart, Teri Cregger, Mallory Esch, Jaime Chellis, Melissa Davis, Matt Trzeciak; *second row* – Abi Smith, Kristin Sausser, Sara McGuire, Brandi Suder, Drew Cool, Chelsea Binder, Janie Cronstrom, Chris Lagona, Jesse Francek, Amanda Rahkola, Blair Clemmens, Bailey Leasher, Alexia Torres, Sheral Taylor; third row – Brittney Parsons, Amber Phillips, Trisha Winters, Matt Foster, Jamie Jeffers, Michael Formsma, Tim Hadley, Josh Kappa, Shane O'Connor, Kyle Linquist, Patrick Bollinger, Samantha VanHorn, Jen Veit, Perry Cunningham; *back row* - Stephanie K., Eric Nartken, Jordan Goldner, Jason Horrocks, Casey Bollinger, Erron Sanders, Chris Charnes and Brad Sweet.

The original Vic's Supermarket.

316 North Mission Street – The small grocery store at the southeast corner of Mission and Lincoln streets was originally Loyd Honeywell's "Honey's Hunk and Chunk" meat market, the first location of Vic's Super Market, now Ric's. At the right is the beginning of construction of the brick building which would house an expanded Vic's Supermarket at 314 North Mission until a move to new quarters at 705 South Mission in the early 1960s. Still on the site in 2010, the building contains: Computers Sales and Service, Cyber's Place, Farmers Insurance Group, Hall of Heros, Shoe Repair, Sports Addix, and Tropical Fish, as well as apartments upstairs.

Above, in a 1947 Vic's ad is staff: Ruth Erler, Ruth Ball, Edna Ervin, Victor Erler (owner), Keith Scott, Woody Allen, Roy Hughes, Rodney Phillips, Lyle Bristol, Carrol Van Ommeren and Albert Clevenger.

Gould Drug Company original Mt. Pleasant Location on Mission.

502 North Mission Street. Originally one of the location evolutions of the Fortino Food Market the northeast corner of Crosslanes and Mission Streets was home to Gould Rexall Drugs from the early 1950s *(above)* until moving to the larger Giant Super Market building *(now Family Video)* at 317 North Mission in the 1970s.

Don Gould later sold Gould Drug Company to Perry Drugs. The former Gould site at Mission and Crosslanes streets, after housing Four Seasons Windows and Siding for about a decades, has been occupied by Grafx Central *(below)* since the late 1990s.

Old-towners remember the Scotty/ Agnes's Wonderland Restaurant on Mission.

700 North Mission Street - The Scotty Restaurant, *above* during 1947 curbing and paving of the new US-27 four-lane "super highway" work, was built in 1937. Helen and Laurence Warren owned the Scotty Restaurant at this location from 1944 to 1948. Phyllis Stavely Bonstelle claims she made her first hamburger there in 1951 for her uncle. Later the Scotty was owned by Jerry McCord, who went on to built the Avalon Bar east of town. Under McCord's ownership, The Scotty was among Mt. Pleasant's first "open after the bars close" diners. Agnes McDonald bought the building and operated Agnes' Wonderland Diner from 1977 until 2002, right.
. In 2005, the building was razed to allow for a strip mall, anchored by Aaron's Sales.

The Green Spot.

808 North Mission Street at the southeast corner of Mission and Pickard streets was the site of Fred Phillips original Green Spot Bar, where owner Fred Phillips was on hand to pour a cold one, *left*.

In 2010, the Green Spot Pub, *below*, owned for many years by Jerry Sheahan, is thriving under Michael Faulkners ownership. If you want a St. Patrick's Day parking place, you better get it by March 1st.

"Hafer's Corner" at Pickard and Mission.

The 1930-era photo above, looking south at the corner of Pickard and Mission streets, shows some of the Hafer Oil Company employees and the Hafer truck fleet. Standing in front of the building, left to right are: John J. Hafer; Floyd Burgess; Roy D. Hafer; Otis Methner; and Gordon Armstrong. The top floor of Kinney School peeks through the trees behind the building and the billboard on the southwest corner, left middle, occupying the lot where Olson's Tire Company is now located.

Hafer Hardware store was bulldozed out of existence in May, 2008. near the northwest corner of Mission and Pickard streets in Mt. Pleasant to allow room for construction of a Walgreen drugstore. The fall of Hafer Hardware brought an end to 82 years of having the Hafer name connected to that corner. According to the Isabella Copunty Genealogical Society book *ISABELLA COUNTY MICHIGAN; Families and History 2003*, Roy D. Hafer and his wife Florence purchased the property in 1926 and built a house there, opening a full-service gasoline filling station on the corner a year later. Hafer Oil Company also delivered gas, fuel oil, kerosene and other petroleum related products to local farmers, homeowners and oil drilling companies in Central Michigan. Their delivery service to oil drilling companies dropped into high gear after the discovery of the Mt. Pleasant oil field east of town on the Isabella/Midland county line, where the Hafers built another filling station at the site of today's Oil City. In the late 1950s, Hafer Oil Company left the gasoline business, leasing the building to the snowmobile dealership of Hafer Hardware next door. In 1981, the gas station site was sold, the station and house demolished and the Flap Jack Restaurant was built there, later to become Fillmore's Restaurant until recent demolition. Just north of the corner on the west side of Mission Street, a full sevice hardware was started in 1947 by John J. Hafer and his stepfather Gordon Jones. In 1950, John D. Hafer took over the entire building and expanded the hardware business in addition to becoming a large Ski Doo brand snowmobile dealer. John Hafer retired in 1983, selling the business (which retained the Hafer name until closing earlier this year) to Glen Irwin.

The hardware has since closed.

"Hafer's Corner" at Pickard and Mission continued.

903 North Mission Street. Roy D. Hafer and his wife Florence purchased the property in 1926 and built a house there, opening a full-service gasoline filling station on the corner a year later *(above)*. Hafer Oil Company also delivered gas, fuel oil, kerosene and other petroleum related products to local farmers, homeowners and oil drilling companies in Central Michigan. Their delivery service to oil drilling companies dropped into high gear after the discovery of the Mt. Pleasant oil field east of town on the Isabella/Midland county line, where the Hafers built another filling station at the site of today's Oil City. In the late 1950s, Hafer Oil Company left the gasoline business, leasing the building to the snowmobile dealership of Hafer Hardware next door. In 1981 the gas station site was sold, the station and house demolished and the Flap Jack Restaurant was built there, later to become Filmore's Restaurant *(right)* until 2008 demolition. Just north of the corner on the west side of Mission Street, a full sevice hardware was started in 1947 by John J. Hafer and his stepfather Gordon Jones. John Hafer retired in 1983, selling the business *(which retained the Hafer name until 2008 closing)* to Glen Irwin. Mt. Pleasant's second Walgreen's location *(below)* opened on the site in 2009.

Site of one of Mt. Pleasant's earliest 24-hour eateries evolved into one of South Mission's oldest family-owned businesses.

406 South Mission - In 1958, Dale Jarrett bought the building above, that for many years housed the White Spot Restaurant *(the author has been unable to locate a photo of the White Spot)*, an all night eatery known to local residents by the more familiar title: "the greasy spoon". Apologies to any surviving owners, unflattering as that may be, about a dozen of the author's contemporaries, when questioned while this address was being researched, didn't know where the White Spot was but readily admitted having partaken of late night coffee at the place they knew by the other name.

In 2013, *left*, the greatly expanded jewery business continues under family ownership with Dale's son Mike at the helm. with the old White Spot building site part of the parking lot,

McFarlane Dairy, coolest place in town when Mission was US 27.

424 South Mission Street was the site of Hubert Brainerd's Dairy, outgrowth of his Orchard Hill Dairy Farm, then Chase's Dairy, inset above. Brainerd's daughter Margaret married Virginian Doug McFarlane in joined her father's growing dairy business. They built a processing plant and opened a dairy bar.

Douglas McFarlane bought the business 1942, operating it as Brainerd's until 1948 when the name changed to McFarlane Dairy, *above*.

The dairy bar in the main building, called Chase's for a time, was legendary for it's ice cream concoctions, including a banana split that is still a subject in Mt. Pleasant nostalgic conversations. McFarlane sold the business in 1968 to McDonalds Dairy of Flint, Michigan. *Below*, the address has been the site of the Firehouse Five Car Wash since the mid-1970s.

Honeywell's Market known for personal service.

The 706-712 South Mission Street location now occupied by Domino's Pizza and a carwash, *below right,* was once occupied by a butcher shop and grocery store. Melvin "Dutch" Honeywell, *above left,* and his wife Philomena bought the store at 712 South Mission from Carl and Esthe Huber in 1947. Honeywell doubled the size of the building in 1947 and held a grand opening later that year, *above right,* with one side dedicated to groceries and the other side the original meat market. He also added two aprtments upstairs, one of which he occupied with his family for three years. Dutch Honeywell, *right foreground in the left photo below, with Rodney Graham, another butcher in the right background with with a pair of unidentified customers,* bought cattle and hogs from local farmers and various stockyards, did his own slaughtering and butchering, then selling the fresh meat in his store. Honeywell's was a family affair, with Dutch and Philomena's son Bob running the slaughterhouse at 4425 East River Road and daughters Shirley and Betty working in the store while John Moore managed the grocery department. Ill health caused Honeywell to sell the business in 1955 and the building was demolished in the late 1960s.

Vintage photos and information about the store were furnished by Mt. Pleasant's Shirley (Honeywell) Sheppard.

Sharrar's Shell Station recognized in national magazine.e

718 South Mission Street, at the southwest corner of Mission and High streets, was the location of Jack E. Sharrar's Jack's Shell service station, festooned for the holidays in this 1957 photograph. Sharrar was the subject of an April, 1958, article in Shell Oil Company's retail dealer's magazine, *Shell Progress, entitled* "Top Man on Mission Street". Cited for the cleanliness of his services station, Sharrar (shown with a customer right) said "We don't set aside any particular time for cleaning up. All spare time is clean-up time."

In those pre-expressway times, Mission Street was U.S. 27, with 26 gasoline service stations in a 16 block stretch. Sharrar, with five years Shell experience at the time, was the top dealer on the "Gasoline Alley" 30,000 gallons of gasoline per month, rising to 43,000 gallons a month in the summer. Many of his customers were tourists, the article said, on their way to the Upper Peninsula and drawn by the "Free Shell Touring Service: sign and Sharrar's spotless station.

In 2013, the location is still a Shell gasoline self-service filling station and convenience store.

The author is grateful to Dr. Jack F. Sharrar of San Francisco's American Conservatory Theater for sharing, by e-mail, these pictures and the article with me …. and now with you.

Jon's Drive-in a perennial favorite since 1957.

1030 South Mission – Longing for the good old days, when you could eat in your car with the radio blasting as your favorite squeeze checked out who was cruising Mission Street? Miss those days …. well, they're still here.

Jon's Country Burgers drive-in restaurant opened by John P. Spiris June 27, 1957, on the northwest corner of Mission and Bellows streets. There were 28 parking spaces alongside two-way speakers where you could order your favorites and there are still 28 spaces where you can do the same.

After an electrical fire in 2000 caused the restaurant to close from April to September, the building was emptied and reconstructed faithful to the original décor inside but with a new sign outside. About the only other thing that has changed since the place opened is the ownership, Jon's is now owned by the founder's son, Jon Spiris, and managed by his son, Mike Spiris, making it three generations of the family serving the same number of generations of Mt. Pleasantites. Would you like fries with that?

1958 photo of brand-new Rowe Hall shows sparsely populate Mission Street south of Bellows.

The brand-new Rowe Hall, *above*, was built in 1958 at the extreme northeast corner of the Central Michigan College Campus, near the southeast corner of Mission and Bellows Streets. The College Elementary School, east wing of the building, closed and was converted to offices in the early 1970s and the former school gymnasium (at the "V" of the building) became home to Central's Museum of Natural History, still operating there. The flat part of the east wing, left, was decimated by fire June 19, 1998. Note two-lane Mission Street (US 127) just left of the east wing. That's the State Highway Department building, now the Michigan Special Olympics offices, with the small chimney, dedicated in 1939, just right of Mission Street with the house across the street at 1143 South Mission the birthplace of Mt. Pleasant's former New Yorker children's clothing store owner Jack Karr.

THE MORNING SUN - JUNE 8, 2011

C & O maintains an image.

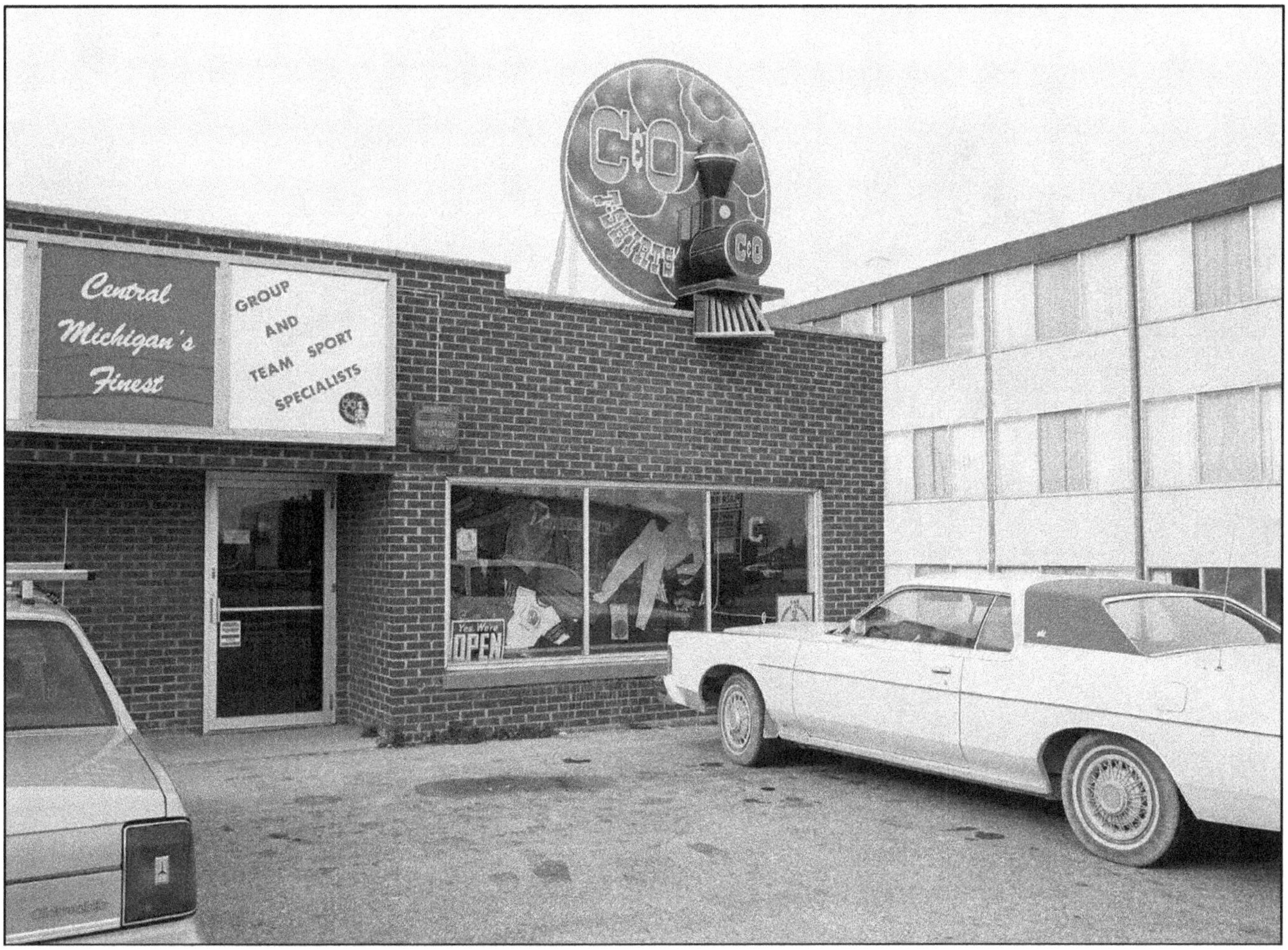

1530 South Mission Street - After humble beginnings in a small building at 711 East Bellows just east behind Jon's Drive-in, C & O T-Shirts moved to their present location in 1981 *(above)*. In 2010, as C & O Sportswear, the business boasts expanded merchandise selection, upgraded equipment, and modernized Western Island Apartments neighbor.

(Top photo by William McEwan, bottom photo by Jack R. Westbrook.)

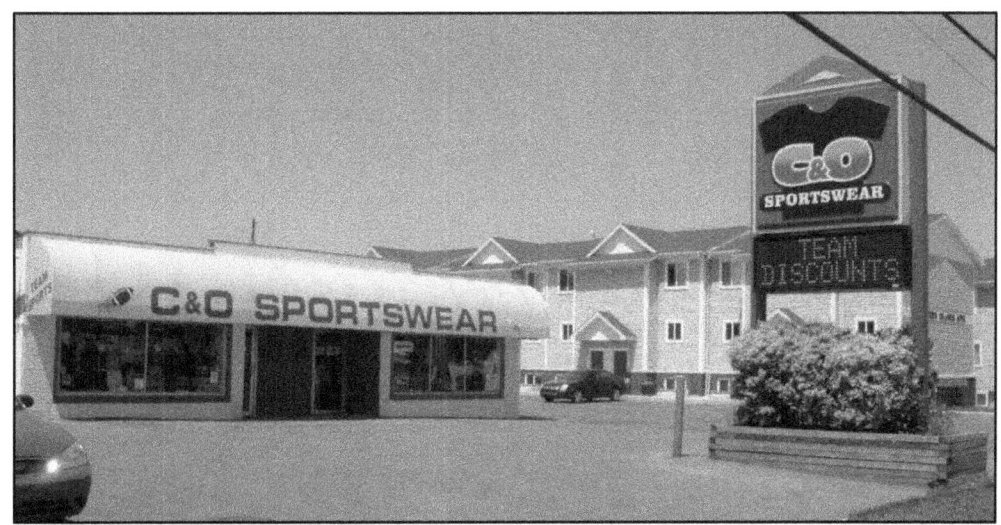

THE MORNING SUN - JUNE 15, 2011

Second generation of Silverberg's shine on South Mission.

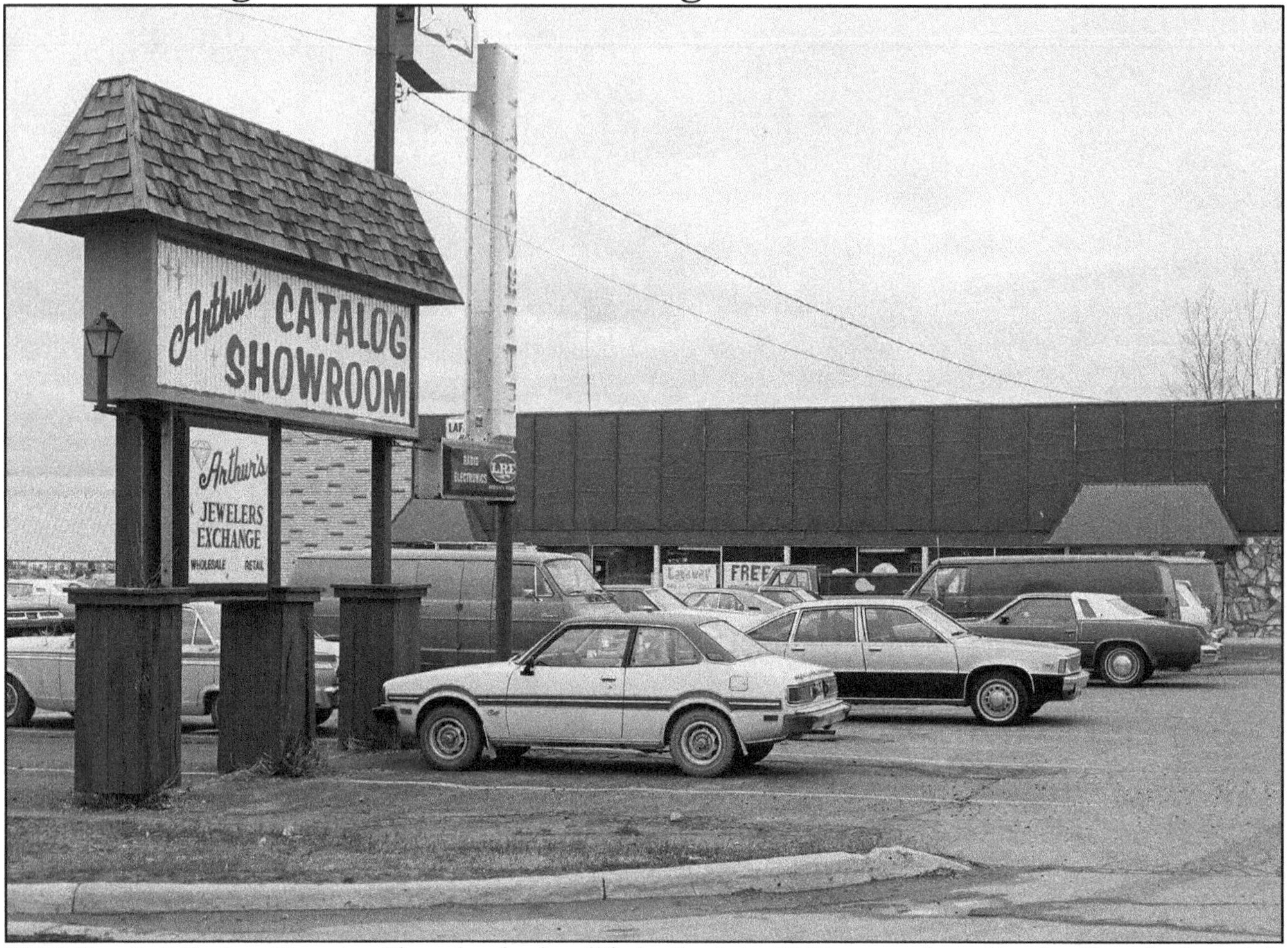

1805 South Mission Street - Since beginning life in the late 1950s as a short-lived roller skating rink, this building has been occupied by business enterprises of the Silverberg family since the early 1960s, when Arthur Silverberg opened Dart Discount, the first general merchandise *(with emphasis on clothing)* discount retail operation in Mt. Pleasant. The operation evolved to meet changing marketing conditions to become Arthur's Catalogue Showroom and Arthur's Jeweler's Exchange *(above in 1980),* then Arthur's Wholesale Distributing later. Today, *below*, Steve Silverberg continues the two generation family tradition at the location with S. Silverberg Finer Jewelers. ***(Top photo by William McEwan and bottom photo by Jack R. Westbrook.)***

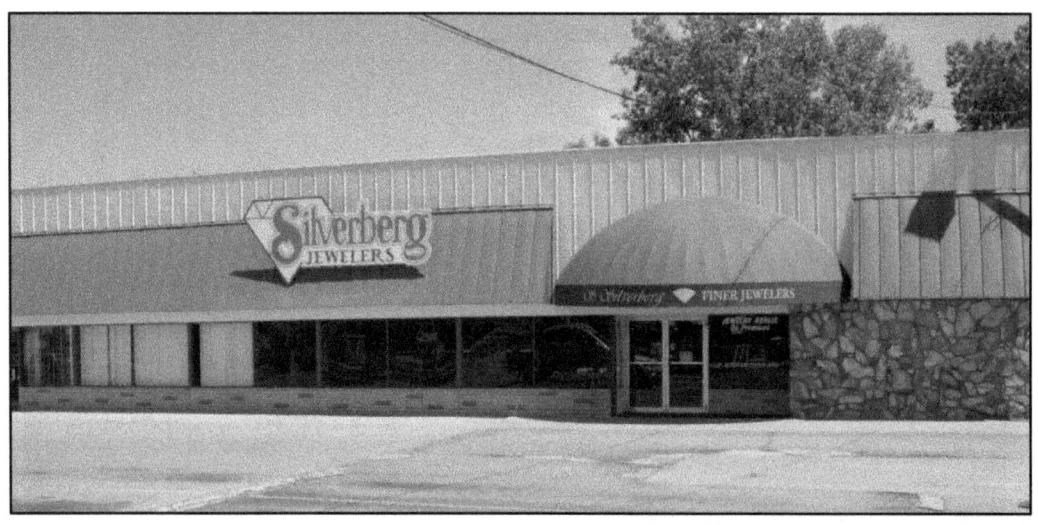

Northeast corner of Broomfield & Mission has serviced motorists for decades.

1911 South Mission Street – The northeast corner of Mission and Broomfield roads, *above*, was for many years a gasoline service station with tourist cabins out behind. When motorists came to Mt. Pleasant from the south on two-lane U.S. 27, these were the first accomodations they encountered. In 1964, Lyle and Harlan "Bones" Hall bought the property from Albert Schertel. The Halls operated from this location until building a new service station at 1620 S. Mission in 1964.

Northeast corner of Broomfield & Mission has serviced motorists for decades (continued).

On the previous page, the Hall Brothers wrecker is shown, not necessarily because it was a unique piece of equipment but in the background, *left*, is the home of Ken Helber, at 1912 South Mission Road, owner of Log Cabin Record Shop, *right*, at 1908 South Mission, a Mt. Pleasant institution for decades, until the early 1970s.

1911 South Mission Street– The northeast corner of Mission and Broomfield roads, above, was for many years a gasoline service station with tourist cabins out behind. When motorists came to Mt. Pleasant from the south on two-lane U.S. 27, these were the first accomodations they encountered.

Since this corner was featured in this space last week, Anne and Don Griffith's postcard collection has yeided an earlier picture of the location when it was Schlafley Tourist Cabins, *above*.

In 1959, Curtis "Ike" and Harlan "Bones" Hall leased the property from Lyle Smith who had purchased it from Albert Schlafley. The Halls operated from this location until building a new service station at 1620 S. Mission in 1964.

Today the site is the location of a Blodgett Oil Shell service station.

Pleasant Lanes once "way out on the country".

2000 South Mission Street – Other early business pioneers on then South Mission Road, were Dick and Wilma Anderson, who in 1950 built their Pleasant Lane bowling alley "clear out in the wilds" of Broomfield and Mission, *above*. Suddenly Mt. Pleasant has two bowling alleys. one over a storefront on South Main and this state of the art facility. Automatic pinsetters were years away when the author hand set pins for the late leagues in the early 50s. The walk home to the West Side through the dark of the field from Broomfield and Mission to Preston and Washington, where the first street light north was located … Washington south of Preston holding only a few residents, railroad tracks and three migrant worker summer season only occupied houses … was punctuated only by the occasional stumble over holes in the then open field.

That field is now paved and lighted and clustered with Central Michigan University buildings.

Pleasant Lanes closed in the mid-1960s, trumped by the more modern facilities of Chippewa Lanes at 1200 South Mission.

In 2010, *below*, Wayside Central and O'Kelly's Pub occupy the address.

AND WITH THIS, WE HAVE BOWLED THE LAST FRAME OF THIS SET.
THANK YOU FOR YOUR INTEREST AND ATTTENTION!

ABOUT THE AUTHOR

JACK R. WESTBROOK is a Mt. Pleasant, Michigan, resident, retired Managing Editor of the Michigan Oil & Gas News magazine and author of four previous historical photo review books for Arcadia Publishing Company: *MICHIGAN OIL & GAS* (2006); *MT. PLEASANT THEN and NOW* (2006); *CENTRAL MICHIGAN UNIVERSITY* (2007); and *ISABELLA COUNTY (Michigan) 1859-2009* (2008). He has self-published: *YESTERDAY'S SCHOOL KIDS OF ISABELLA COUNTY,* with co-author historian/genealogist Sherry Sponseller (2009); *ANOINTED WITH OIL: MY JOURNEY WITH FAITH FROM THE OILFIELDS OF MICHIGAN TO THE LEGISLATIVE HALLS OF WASHINGTON DC and BACK AGAIN*, by C. John Miller as told to Jack R. Westbrook (2010); *THE BIG PICTURE BOOK OF MT. PLEASANT, MICHIGAN: Yesteryears to 2010* (2010); *MICHIGAN NATURAL RESOURCES TRUST FUND* (2011); AT HOME IN EARLIER MT. PLEASANT, MICHIGAN (2012); MID-MICHIGAN HISTORY: THE MT.PLEASANT AREA'S PAST AS SEEN IN THE MORNING SUN & MT. PLEASANT MONTHLY MAGAZINE PHOTO FEATURES (2013).

Westbrook's first work of fiction, *KAISA*: A NOVEL OF MICHIGAN'S COPPER MINING & OIL AND GAS EXPLORATION AND PRODUCTION INDUSTRIES; CALUMET; HOLLAND; MT. PLEASANT; MACKINAC ISLAND AND JEKYLL ISLAND, GEORGIA was published in August of 2013.

KAISA: A Novel of Michigan's Copper Mining & Oil & Gas Exploration Industries; Calumet; Holland; Mt. Pleasant; Mackinac Island; and Jekyll Island, Georgia

A sweeping tale of the 1913 Keweenaw Peninsula copper miner's strike to the 1930s oil boomtown of Mt. Pleasant, Michigan, Mackinac Island, Michigan, and Jekyll Island, Georgia, in 1942 **312 pages - $16.95**

MICHIGAN OIL AND GAS

A photo history of Michigan's oil and natural gas exploration and production history from 1925 discovery to modern times to see the state become 12th largest gas and 17th largest crude oil producer of the 34 petroleum producing states. **128 pages - $21.99**

MT. PLEASANT THEN and NOW

Since 1860, Mt. Pleasant has been a center for Native American culture, lumbering, oil and gas exploration and production, collegiate learning and retail shopping. 1800s to 1950s photos are compared to modern photo views of the same locations. **98 pages - $21.99**

CENTRAL MICHIGAN UNIVERSITY

A photographic profile of the growth of Michigan's 4th largest university from 1892 founding to modern times, with profiles of the persons for whom Mt. Pleasant Campus buildings were named for academic reasons. **128 pages - $19.99.**

ISABELLA COUNTY: 1859-2009

The official sesquicentennial book celebrating in photographs Isabella County's journey from river side village to robustly diversified commerce and education center.
128 pages - $21.99

YESTERDAY'S SCHOOL KIDS OF ISABELLA COUNTY

An in-depth photographic look at 215 photographs of schools and kids as they were in their yesteryear school years. If a structure still stands, it's photograph appears in the book. Book comes with an 11x14 Isabella County map of standing structure locations indicated and described.
240 pages - $25.00

The BIG Picture Book of Mt. Pleasant, Michigan

The most comprehensive photo history of Mt. Pleasant's growth from lumbering outpost to city ever published. Introduces the newcomer to Mt. Pleasant's heritage while providing the longtime resident with hours of nostalgic photo memories. **336 pages - $25.00**

AT HOME IN EARLIER MT. PLEASANT, MICHIGAN

Travel by photos through the streets of the historic core of this lumber/oil/university city in the center of Michigan and meet some of the residents who have added colorful threads to the tapestry of the community's past with 396 photographs. **264 pages - $25.00.**

SEE BOOK DESCRIPTIONS ON OPPOSITE PAGE

JACK R. WESTBROOK BOOK ORDER FORM

Please enter my order for the following books (descriptions on reverse side)

$_____ (# of copies of MICHIGAN OIL & GAS x $21.99)

$_____ (# of copies of MT. PLEASANT THEN & NOW x $21,99)

$_____ (# of copies of CENTRAL MICHIGAN UNIVERSITY x $19.99)

$_____ (# of copies of ISABELLA COUNTY 1859-2009 x $21.99)

$_____ (# of copies of YESTERDAY'S SCHOOLKIDS OF ISABELLA COUNTY x $25.00

$_____ (# of copies of THE BIG PICTURE BOOK OF MT. PLEASANT x $25.00)

$_____ (# of copies of MICHIGAN NATURAL RESOURCES TRUST FUND x $ 19.95)

$_____ (# of copies of AT HOME IN EARLIER MT. PLEASANT MI x 25.00)

$_____ (# of copies of KAISA: A NOVEL OF MICHIGAN AND GEORGIA x $16.95

$_____ (# of copies of MID-MICHIGAN HISTORY x $12.25)

$_____ (TOTAL BOOK COST)

$_____ sales tax TOTAL BOOK COST x 6%)

$_____ shipping & handling: 1 book-$3.50; 2 books- $4.50; 3 books or more, FREE Shipping

I enclose $_____ TOTAL - for IMMEDIATE shipping

------MASTERCARD _____ VISA _____ AMERICAN EXPRESS _____ DISCOVER

NAME ON CARD _____ NUMBER _____ _____ _____
EXP_____ SEC. NO _____

Name _____ Phone _____

Address _____ City _____ State__
ZIP_____

Inscription for personal autographs _____
(use separate sheet if necessary)
Make checks payable to Jack R. Westbrook
Send orders to: BOOKS, Jack R. Westbrook ORSB , PO Box 16, Mt. Pleasant MI 48804-0016